MY ROAD TO SOBRIETY

FINDING SUCCESS THE HARD-WAY

Front Cover produced by Englewood Camera with special thanks to Brandy Brown

MIKE MCCARTHY

SCRIPTOR HOUSE
THE EPITOME OF GREATNESS

Scriptor House LLC
2810 N Church St Wilmington, Delaware, 19802
www.scriptorhouse.com
Phone: +1302-205-2043

Front Cover produced by Englewood Camera with special thanks to Brandy Brown

Paperback ISBN: 979-8-88692-243-1
eBook ISBN: 979-8-88692-244-8
Hardback ISBN: 979-8-88692-308-7

MY ROAD TO SOBRIETY

FINDING SUCCESS THE HARD-WAY

MIKE MCCARTHY

FOREWORD

My Road to Sobriety

I feel honoured that I was asked to write the foreword for Michael's story. Like Michael, I have years of sobriety, and years discovering old beliefs and habits that didn't work for a sober lifestyle. I kept looking for people and pathways that would help me in that search. I learned to share in AA meetings, share with my sponsors, join various support groups, and learn that trying to help others helped me. I told my story at meetings, becoming quite comfortable doing it. The punch line of my talk would be, "My dad was an Irish, Catholic cop, to say he was an Alcoholic was a redundancy!"

Things were going so well that I said yes to doing a talk on spirituality at an AA Conference in Sault Ste. Marie, Ontario. Things didn't go well there of course. It was a large group on a Saturday morning. I froze up. I never said a word! Was quite sure I was going to pass out. I stood there frozen until people started to line up to hug me and let me know I was ok. I discovered another fear I had that wasn't true. Public speaking didn't kill me. I joined Toastmasters shortly after to support me in this area. AA and Toastmasters are both groups that help people through their fears. I continued to search, leading me to do a lot of soul-searching and forgiveness work. I eventually became a minister with a small church and spent time doing spiritual counselling. I have tried to incorporate the lessons I learned throughout the rest of my life.

Michael and I met in grade school and bonded over sports and minor acts of rebellion in a rather strict school system. I was in a class with Michael's sister Mary one year ahead of Michael. However, it was a small school and easy to get to know the students in the other grades. By the time we got to high school, we often walked home for lunch in a group too. Looking back it's easy to see that we tended to form a group of friends with common themes. The themes were often influenced by alcohol and family secrets leading to frustration and anger issues. During football, basketball, and hockey (for me) season, we got to work off some of the angry energy in a competitive environment. It wasn't enough.

It got worse after high school. That's when we started to drink to excess. It was easy for us to get carried away when we drank. We all thought we were being jovial and hilarious. But people could see trouble coming when we walked through the door. It's a good thing we had that tight bond because I don't know if I would have liked us very much. We were hurting young men unaware of why we hurt. I am very thankful people are willing to support us who are unaware of the pain we are carrying.

Mike leads the reader through multiple examples of the fear and pain that can be shared behind the closed doors of our family home. He also gives examples of how he compensated for those emotions. He also shows how his way of dealing with pain affected his life. He takes us step by step through the process involved in his ability to surrender his defences and find help in sobriety. He sets an example for how to begin a life-long path of healing. He took his unique path to get sober. His mom took a different approach. Both worked. Mike shows us that sobriety works. Sobriety opens the door for us to reclaim our innocence and help bring us some peace. Sobriety is a tool that allows us to continue the work that needs to be done. It allows us the freedom to get in touch with feelings and emotions that need to be released. Sobriety can open us to love and support those in need. Sobriety helps us love our families and ourselves.

Again, I thank my friend, Mike, for having the courage to share his journey. I am proud to call him my friend and fellow traveller on the road to healing.

Bless you, Rev. Peter Campbell

THE SERENITY PRAYER

The Serenity Prayer serves as a focal point for the very spirit of AA, anchoring its members to its quintessential teachings about surrender and acceptance.

God grant me the serenity to accept the things I cannot change,

The courage to change the things I can,

And the wisdom to know the difference

TABLE OF CONTENTS

INTRODUCTION

Since I broke my anonymity of my alcoholism with my Facebook posting, many people have urged me to tell the whole story. And those who have lived a life anonymously like myself, will know how difficult that could be. Over a year ago, I wanted to celebrate my 50th year of sobriety, and this time more openly. When my 50-year coin came in the mail, I then decided to post my testimony on Facebook so my friends would know what I thought was the most major accomplishment in my life after the birth of my three children. So many friends responded with congratulations and just wonderful things to say. I was so appreciative, but the strangest thing occurred. Friends of friends of friends contacted me on Facebook. People I never heard of before, people I just didn't know, writing to me and telling me how my story gave them a bounce and encouragement, and a renewed belief they too can find sobriety and turn their life around. Many were married and some were divorced, some were young in their early 20s, and a few had crashed on their recovery program and started drinking again, but needed to find a way back in. It was unbelievable, it was. So after the success of my first two books, 'The Sounds and Smells of My Childhood,' I thought for many months, long and hard about opening up my soul. My question was, "How should I do it"? My purpose and prayer became very simple. Please Lord, "find at least one individual, at least one soul who is fighting that damn sickness and addiction of alcoholism and let them read this book to find hope, joy, and peace, and their own road to sobriety."

My story has many dark moments, but they all are real events. There were times of laughter and lots of tears, but throughout, there was an addiction building slowly within me, aiming at ruining my life. While I was growing professionally, and learning new things in my career, and becoming a rising star in my profession. My life was being destroyed by something I had inherited, but one I could have defeated early on, but I gave in to it.

So my hope is I can still believe in 'The Power Of One.' One person, one thought, or one new idea, can bring some change to anything. One Individual bitten by the addiction to alcohol is out there, and I hope my book finds that person. If I can achieve that, then giving up my anonymity will have been worth it, and my story should be told and needs to be told as something of value. I hope you find it meaningful.

CHAPTER ONE

Happy Birthday

On October 19, 2023, my life turned the clock to that glorious age of 75. Seventy-five years old. I thought to myself, and said" Wow" but still I just couldn't believe it. All of my family, and several friends wrote to me and called to wish me well on that great day. My sisters, Mary and Kathy, and Jean, my sister-in-law, kept up my Mother's tradition of calling me and singing the "Happy Birthday song." My younger brother, Tim, 61 himself, enjoyed reminding me I was much older than himself and complimented me when he said, "You were supposed to be dead at thirty", and you're still kicking that can." "I'm glad you're still around, I love you, Mike."

Then my kids, my nephews and my nieces chipped in, wishing me well and to enjoy the day. My wife, Judy, God love her, for my present, brought me back to Ireland, and we enjoyed our time visiting with family and friends. It's like going back home. It's felt like that since my first visit in 1972. Walking in the Glen of Aherlow and standing on the shores of West Clare, ignites something special in me and speaks to my soul.

One family of importance in my life has been the O'Connors. The O'Connor family from Tipperary Ireland with their older sister Marie. She was born the same day as myself, but a year earlier., We have celebrated our day together for years. We met 52 years ago while I was hitchhiking around Ireland. I was walking and thumbing for a ride, on the old Cahir-Bansha road in County Tipperary. She was a history teacher, coming home early from school in Cahir. She was sick and drove the old road home. Sure enough, she stopped and picked up this Irish Yank. I was hitchhiking to the town of Tipperary to visit the gravesite of Sean Tracy. He was an Irish rebel, fighting for Irish Independence. He was killed in Dublin during the Irish troubles 1918-1921 with England, and buried in the town of Tipperary. She remarked immediately, "What on earth does an Irish Yank know about Sean Tracy"? I told her, he was my boyhood hero, and I knew and studied his life and his strong commitment to an independent Ireland. She told me about her Grandfather. dug the gravesite for Sean Tracy. So began our wonderful relationship.

The Irish Author Tomas O'Suileabhan in his book 'Twenty Years of Growing' said all life falls into four patterns. The First, Twenty years of Growing; the Second, Twenty years of Learning; the Third, Twenty years of Knowing; and the Fourth, Twenty Years of Declining. Returning home to Denver on the plane from Ireland. I began to think about the many roads of my life, especially my early teenage years and early twenties. That special period of my life that took me through the scare of the Cuban Missile Crisis, through Catholic High School, falling in love for the first time, and on through University, falling in love for the second time, passing through the peaks and turmoil of the Civil Rights marches, experiencing the Assassinations of our political and religious leaders, including our first Catholic president, and the horrors of the VietNam war. The Road to Wisdom they say, comes with age, and I thank God he opened that door for me. I thought during my reflection on my youth, I wished I had this knowledge when I needed it the most. My Road to Sobriety which defines me to this day may have had a softer landing or not exist at all. You see, I am a recovered alcoholic. I just celebrated my 51st anniversary of sobriety, and when I received my 50-year coin, I was elated and filled with pride. In my mind, it is the most beautiful coin I have ever seen. So while I celebrated my anonymous accomplishment, I began to look back to where and how it ended, and how it began.

CHAPTER TWO

The Ending

On December 24, 1972, I drove from the Soo to visit my family in Marquette, to celebrate Christmas. It was that time of year, to enjoy a great Christmas Eve dinner made by my mother. My brothers and sisters would be there, and my Father too. We were a very close family, where love, loyalty, and forgiveness were practised, preached and lived. And of course, there was always the drink. There was plenty of laughter and of course some great food fights and arguments. We all chipped in and sang a few songs together, which we always did and enjoyed as we aged and grew up. It was great listening to the voices of John and Kathy, while Mary and I were good participants, and even our little brother Tim, now 8 years old, knew the songs. Thinking back on that trip now, it sounds like it would be a simple drive, and it should be. It's just 3 Hours in length if you don't have any car problems, or get caught in a good Seney stretch winter storm. The Seney stretch was a highway length of 25 miles of straight open highway. It was an open stretch where the winter winds and snow would blind you. The drive took me over 8 hours to get there and the worst part is, I missed my mother's entire dinner. But I managed to stop by every bar or saloon along the 180-mile drive. There were 17 places in all, and I must admit I enjoyed a drink or two at every one of these joyous establishments, celebrating Christmas.

I just turned 24, and at that time I knew I wasn't well. I was very ill. I was a very heavy drinker, with two ulcers. I wasn't eating regularly, but I was drinking at least 4 six packs a day. That seemed to be all that kept me going. I was vomiting and passing blood. The more I drank, the momentarily seemed to stop everything but heal nothing. Then, Hell itself broke loose., the stomach pain worsened, the vomiting started back, and I was experiencing more urine in the blood. But, what my alcoholic mind kept telling me was, I was ok. I thought it made sense, as crazy as that sounds, despite my apparent decline. I got home to my parents at their Park Street location at about 10 p.m. on Christmas Eve. I was very inebriated, which is a nice way to say I was very drunk. I didn't mind about my condition, as my whole family got used to drunkenness at Christmas time. My father set that stage for us for many years. Although I got over it years before, I felt there was nothing to fear, and no need to worry about anything. But I did feel bad about not being there for my Mother's great dinner.

After an hour of catching up with family and my sisters' and brothers', my Father walked me into the kitchen, where my Mother was sitting drinking a cup of coffee. She put me up a small meal that I immediately vomited. She then brewed up a pot of tea, and poured me a cup, and kept pouring and filling it. Then, came the old McCarthy remedy. Out of the fridge came the MaaIox and Mylanta to calm and coat the stomach, and some Butabel to numb the ulcer pain. While all this was going on I was getting lectured by my Dad. He demanded I quit the drinking as it was "killing me", He said. I was trying to make light of it all. I yelled into the front room to have John and Tim come to the kitchen and sing, 'The Wild Rover Song' with me. We started to sing the song, and then my Mother erupted and chased John out of the kitchen to leave for home, and for Tim to get to bed. So, my Father and Mother talked to me, until 2 am on Christmas morning. I knew that I just needed to listen to both of them, as I respected and loved my parents. So I planned to show them I was listening, and as soon as I could, I would drive back home to the Soo right after Christmas. As I said earlier, I truly believed in my Dad and deeply loved my Mother, and I knew the rules of loyalty to the family, and our history of alcohol abuse by my father. Having a Father that's bigger than life itself to most kids can be intimidating, but I was never one that was easy to frighten. He wanted his sons to be strong and tough. So of course, I argued back. I told him how I could handle my drinking, even though I was arrested 4 times, for drunk and disorderly conduct, and twice for impaired driving. To me, I wasn't hurting anyone, unlike him, that was my point, and it was working. At least that's how my drunken mind saw it.

My mother was trying her best to be kind and caring, during my yelling match with my father. She kept saying to me, I needed to see a Doctor. She said, "I was in poor health, and I wasn't leaving Marquette until I saw this Irish Doctor by the name of Kevin O'Brien." He was an internal medicine specialist, and she had set up an appointment for me, without me knowing anything about it.

My drinking was becoming a family issue. My Mother knew I would not see any Doctor who was not Irish. So while the intense chat with Dad heated up, and I thought I out-yelled him, he came back into the kitchen. This time holding our family Bible, and his Colt 45, a pearl-handled pistol that he brought home after WWII. There was a long history in my family with that damn pistol, especially with my siblings and myself. It started years ago, first with my brother John, with what we called the "night terror," and even my sister Mary had to face it, and then of course myself. I tried to find humour in it all instead of being frightened. But, I was surprised to see my Father ready to threaten me once again with it. After all, I thought I was 24, not 13. My mother was beside herself and very upset, when Dad pulled his pistol and pointed it at my head. She kept on yelling at him and pleading with me to go to bed, and for Dad to quit acting this way. But Dad was getting more angry with me and he was the sober one. He demanded I swear on the Bible I will quit drinking. I was about ready to walk out when I looked at him with that Colt 45 pistol pointed at my head. He then cocked the gun. He said to me crying, with tears coming down his cheeks, "Mike, I love you." But, you either quit drinking now, and get your ass to the hospital, or I am going to shoot you right here." "And then, I am going to shoot myself, as I'm no good without you." "Now swear on this Holy Bible you will quit." I looked at him, and I told him, "That damn gun doesn't scare me at all Dad." But after two pots of tea and a stomach filled with digestive medication, I took a closer look at him. I believe to this day, especially seeing my Father cry like that, and seeing those tears wash down his cheeks, he was going to do it. He was serious. I thought for a quick minute, and told myself "Let's get out of here Mike, go along with this guy, and give him what he wants, then get your ass back to the Soo." Finally, I said to both of them. "I'll quit, okay? I swear Dad. Mom, I'll go see the Doctor later today, but now, I'm going to bed." I hugged and kissed both of my Mom and Dad and off I went to their guest room. Walking up the stairs a million thoughts rushed through my mind. I was thinking about going to the hospital later on Christmas Day, I was thinking about my poor father and mother going through all of this. I was wondering about this fellow Dr. O'Brien, and how I might work him into my corner. Then a little humour kicked in with an old song by my Father's dear friend Bill Murphy used to sing. It went like this,

'Like Your Dad'

You get more like your Dad every day you young Turk,

You get more like your Dad every day.

Some tricks I have played,

he would say, You young blade.

You get more like your Dad every day.

You know, Looking more clearly at this now, it is still hard to speak openly about it. Although I have told the story several times among my own, at over 300 AA meetings I have attended. As the Irish playwright Sean O'Casey once wrote about the Irish race, "those brilliant, beautiful fools. "Well, that was my Dad. To those who have heard this story, and have felt that my Dad was pretty mean and horrible, I tell them, "No he wasn't, he was showing me how much he loved me, and how he failed me and all my brothers and sisters, and didn't want to see my life ruined."

Off To Meet Dr. O'Brien

Later that Christmas morning, My Mother woke me from my sleep at 10 am, and told me to "get up now and get bacon and eggs, if you can eat. She said, "She'll take me to the Hospital to see Dr O'Brien." She packed some of my old clothes that I kept there when they moved from the Sault to Marquette, and she then told me I would be there in the Hospital for seven days. "Today is important, she said, as Dr O'Brien will give you a series of tests." I didn't realize until then, I was off to a detox unit that my mother had set up. I met with Dr O'Brien, and he was a Boston Irishman. I liked that and I liked him. I was still shaking quite a bit from an evening of heavy drinking. My ulcers were acting up and my stomach was very painful. I knew I needed a morning drink to take care of all of this. But without any drink, and before my Mother and I left, I took a morning Butabel pill and took a big swallow of Mylanta to coat my stomach and stop the stomach pain. I told Dr O'Brien of my Ulcers and that I was passing blood in my urine, and that concerned me. I was of course doing my best to control the conversation. I remember telling him, "I don't need to go into that detox unit", and he just laughed. After about 6 hours of all kinds of medical tests, internal medicine exams, kidney exams, urine tests, x-rays, cat scans, he came to me and reported his findings. He blew up a balloon and put an acidic solution in the balloon as it was filled with air. He then rolled it around a few times, and showed me how this was like my stomach wall, and the acid was similar to mine as I had both a bleeding and peptic ulcer producing acidic reflux. Then all a sudden the balloon popped, in fact it exploded. I was surprised, stunned really, when he told me, "now this is what is going to happen to your stomach Mike." "And all you have to do is continue your drinking." Needless to say, I wasn't expecting such news, and then he said, "you probably can make another 6 months of your life before this happens to you." I was speechless, listening very closely for sure. He then asked me, "Do you want to live, or do you want to continue drinking?" As I said I liked him a lot, and he scared the hell out of me. He explained how I could cure my ulcers, with a proper diet and that I need not worry about the blood in my urine, as my kidney was bruised, probably from a hard fall I'd taken. But, "it was time to detox and dry out from alcohol," or "go ahead and enjoy your death as it will happen very fast with very little to no pain." "You will just bleed to death and go to sleep." I chose to live and off to the detox unit I went.

The Detox Unit

So here I was, Christmas Day, 1972, in a detox unit at Marquette General Hospital in Marquette, Michigan. The staff processed me quickly and professionally. My first session was with two program staff that outlined for me the minimum 7 day stay for detoxification. Although there was a thirty day program, most of those individuals were assigned to go there Instead of spending thirty days in jail. They put me on fruit juices and honey immediately, with no hard food or desert. I didn't mind that too much as I wasn't eating too much anyway, but I must say I loved as much honey as they could give me. They watched closely my stomach issues and gave me gas pills and my Butabel for pain. It was a busy first night and day, as I was meeting with someone all the time. In the early evening at 8 pm, I sat in on my first group therapy meeting and heard new jargon that I never heard before. I was glad to sit back quietly and listen and learn from people who were there for a while. It was interesting hearing their stories as to how each of them got to the hospital program. They seemed sincere and wanted to hear about others and their addictive behavior. I wondered to myself, "Is this place really for me?" On the second day, I was given light toast, some apple juice and a poached egg. Of course honey was again served and I gobbled mine down with toast, and asked for more. I never consumed as much honey in my entire life, and found out it was a much needed dietary replacement to the consumption of alcohol. I was hearing about the twelve steps to alcoholic recovery, and I certainly bought into the fact that I was powerless over alcohol. But I did struggle with the thought I was a drunk, I knew I couldn't handle my drink, but to me an alcoholic was not a drunk. I then recalled my Father and myself leaving Hallesy's Bar in the Soo, and walking out the back door in the alley way, up popped an "older drunken bum" who stopped my Dad and me and wanted some money to ""get something to eat." I told him to move on, but my Dad put his arm around him and gave him $20 and told him to get some food, but not a drink. I told my Dad he was just a drunken bum, and my Dad threw me against the alley fence and said, "don't ever call him that Mike, there is a fine line between him and us, and thank God we're not." "And if not for the grace of God we would be him." I didn't know at the time, but this man, who I called a drunken bum, said that we would actually share a cookie and a cup of tea at a closed AA meeting together just a few years later. I guess what you don't know, won't hurt you. But we became good AA friends, and I heard a new term called, "a sobriety brother." A term that had greater meaning the longer I was sober, and the older I got. There was Tim, Jerry, Jim, Tom, Richard and Tommy. We each shared the same journey of the fight to stay sober and find enjoyment in our sobriety.

I told this story during my private therapy session that same day, and some very intense therapy began as a result. It opened my eyes as to what I needed to do and admit to myself. They began to tell me of what was ahead of me. I still needed to face my own personal challenges and what my body was going to go through these next several days. They made me aware of the withdrawals that I was going to face, as I was a Chronic alcoholic. The fact that my stay in the unit was voluntary meant I could check myself out at any time. So they told me in advance, and it gave me a scare not knowing how serious my withdrawal would be. So sure enough, on the third day, almost 72 Hours after my admission I checked myself out of the Hospital and drove home to the Soo. I called my mother and told her I'm home, and it startled her to say the least, and immediately she asked how I was?

I went home, but first I stopped by our local store and bought plenty of honey, bread to make my toast, eggs, and apple juice. I walked to my home and locked the door. I locked myself in for three days and would not leave. Then I waited for hell to come, and it came like nothing I've ever experienced before. The withdrawals I was expecting were in fact the DT's or better known as the Delirium Tremens. Not to relive my surviving this, but first, it was the sweats, then the chills, then changes to your breathing, but the worst part was having an over stimulated brain. Seeing things that really didn't exist, really frightened me. All of this was frightening enough when other strange animals and ghosts appeared. I prayed and prayed and I know the Blessed Mother was there with me and brought me through this. I emerged from my apartment 72 hours later, and began my new life. Of course there still were challenges, dry drunks , and at times erratic behavior, but the worst had passed. Without the help of several people such as Verna, Alice, Rosie, Ron, Cindy, and my first AA sponsor Jim, I couldn't have made it. I began my new life with the 12 steps as my guidepost. I am still working on them and finding happiness.

CHAPTER THREE

AA Step 8

Make a list of all those you have harmed, and make amends, seeking their forgiveness.

I must say, I have done my best to recall those I've injured and harmed. I have asked for their forgiveness, and expressed how truly sorry I am to have hurt them. If I missed you, the reader, please know how sorry I am. Sometimes even a public apology has meaning.

But there were three people, all women, whom I was at my worst. I need to mention them, not by name as their anonymity is important too. One was an Irish girl, one an Italian girl, and the other my Mother. Both girls were dear friends actually of mine, but it's a horrible truth, how an alcoholic mind and actions destroys those you regard and truly care for. It's taken me years to air my horrible deed to them. I wanted to truly put it out of my mind. I couldn't believe I'd do something so stupid and so hurtful, especially to people I liked. But there is something special about genuine repentance. It takes 10,000 pounds off your shoulders, and you feel alive once more. You never know if things can ever return to normalcy, but trying to do so is the most important thing. If they read this, I can only once again ask for your forgiveness. I am truly sorry for hurting you, for harming you, I want you to believe how sincere I am in asking this of you. I'm truly sorry. Please forgive me. With my Mother during my years of sobriety, I finally woke up to the fact it was her all along that had the solution to my sobriety. My Dad's actions were dramatic and very much like him, he was being his true self. But, it was my mother who had the solution. It was Dr O'Brien. I remember before she died I never asked her for forgiveness. We enjoyed a very loving, strong, and good relationship. I knew I needed to say I was sorry for the harm I caused her. I knew I had deeply hurt her, and so loved her. I sobbed like a child, and the only line she said, "it was all the Holy Mother Mike. Don't ever let her go. You're tied to her now. I love you too."

My Dislike of Authority

One more mention of my past is still very important. As you have read, I had a very strong dislike for those in authority, especially, those in my opinion who abused the authority that was given to them. Only those who earned it, were given my ultimate respect. For me, in my youth and my drinking years, there were the priests, the nuns, and many policemen. and I must say all of this was a direct reflection of my fighting with my Dad during the years of our "night terror".

I was never abused by a priest, but I do believe we had numbers of priests who were missing an egg, in other words they were one egg short of a dozen. They were cunning, and had drinking problems of their own. Their actions did catch up with them, as it was later proven in a legal report from the Marquette diocese as it listed over 12 priests who were involved in my family's schooling and in our religious practice. Lots of shame there. But on one occasion a group of 6 of my friends tried to set up a priest in a sting, and get him reported to the Bishop. We used the confessional as our means to set up the sting. We didn't succeed, but he was caught abusing young kids and later was immediately transferred and defrocked. The whole mess left a very poor taste in my mouth about the abuse, and how my church spent years covering up their sins. And it still burns inside me to this day. But I thank God, for giving me the Jesuit priests and Benedictine priests. They had a sense of spiritual service that definitely I called on during my early years of sobriety.

The Nuns were a special lot. They were supposed to be, Loving, Caring, and great Educators. They were to be Examples of our Blessed Mother I was told. I speak about some of them very kindly and fondly in my other books, as they greatly impacted my life. But, the majority of them loved to rule with an iron fist. They enjoyed their power and demanded respect from children, whether they gave it back or not. I just was not built like that, which is why I never really wanted to go to a Catholic School, it was for John and Mary, not for me. So, for those to whom I didn't like, I either told them directly or showed them. But, the ones I did like and respected, I was just the opposite. I thanked them. It didn't make for an enjoyable experience for attending elementary or secondary education, but I did get a great education. And as I said, I met some great people who remain great friends to this day.

My love or disdain for the Police profession suffered too, at the expense of my childhood experience with my father who really abused his authority. In the East End we had five families whose parents were police officers. Our neighbor Gloria worked in the sheriff's department, and she was great. Just around the corner on Portage was Bobby C, a great Italian kid and a great cop, and a darn good ball player. And on the corner of Spruce Street and Sova Street was Lieutenant Al and his two sons Albert and Ed, both younger police officers. They were a real Police family. I could write about these folks and family all day as they simply saved my life on at least 5 occasions. Before I had my car, on several occasions Lt . Al drove me home after the bars closed, and always said, "take care of yourself Mike."'. We knew this family well and we went to school with Al's daughter Connie. I have called them the Rotary Saints of the East End. What I liked about them all was, they always looked out for the East End boys growing up as kids, trying to keep them out of trouble, right through our teenage years and into our twenties. This was during my drinking years. Another was a Sergeant in the police department, he and his family lived on Maple. He had a strong reputation of being fairly tough himself. Someone you didn't mess with. But he was gracious to kids, and kind. Kids knew him and loved him. Everyone called him by his nickname Hump. He watched over us who lived in the East End and did his share of coaching hockey and boxing. We went to school with his son Pete. He too was an East Ender. Thank God we had all of them, as they earned their respect the hard way and showed people respect. Now I'm sure there were several others, who were respectful and honorable, and we all knew the State Police had better community relations than our own municipal police. At least that's how I felt back then.

My family, and My Mother's prayers kept me standing up. One of the great gifts that happens with a sober life, is eight years later I helped my Father find a new life of sobriety himself. It became a major part of his last five years of his life. The gift was how he and my Mother fell in love all over again. We went to

AA meetings together, and I knew when he introduced himself at the meeting, "hello I'm John, and I'm an alcoholic ", and the members responded "Hi John", I knew we reached a new time in our family relationships. A poem I grew up with now had more meaning, than ever before. It was called,

'Off to Clifden Fair',

He stumbled home from Clifden fair with drunken song, and cheeks aglow,

Yet, there was something in his air that told of Kingship long ago.

I sighed, and endly cried with grief, that one so high, could fall so low.

But he plucked a flower, and sniffed its scent,

and held it toward the sunset sky. Some old sweet rapture through him went,

and kindled in his blood shot eye.

I turned, and endly burned with joy, that one so low, could rise so high.

So fifty one years later, here I am a recovered alcoholic. I'm also a recovered drunk, powerless over alcohol, but I've tried to live a life of helping others and giving back anyway I could, and tried to make mine a life worth living. I've become a human being, at last. But How and Why did it all begin?

CHAPTER FOUR

The Beginning

I was reading recently in The NY Times that there are 48 million Americans suffering from a form of substance abuse. Only 5% are actively in therapy and in various stages of recovery. The three main substance abusers fall into these categories with Alcoholism number one, Opioid addiction number two, and the third, is Sedative addiction.

I was five years old when I first remembered hearing my Uncle Glen and my father arguing in the front room of our apartment. We lived with My grandparents and had a two bedroom unit. There were us four kids, and Mom and Dad. The two of them were both talking very loud and it woke me, when I called out for my mother. She came into our bedroom I shared with my brother and sister. She assured me, John, and Mary, everything will be ok. All of a sudden my Dad punched my Uncle and knocked him through the front window, and he fell into the porch. That was the very first time I heard about both men drinking, and referring to it as, "that damned drink". Of course, Both my mother and grandmother were very angry. But both were more upset with Uncle Glen. I soon learned from both of them, one of the special survival gifts of an alcoholic abused family is that things are always "rosey dosey." In other words, "everything is fine, it's no one else's business but ours, stay loyal to your family, and try to forgive and forget." That was our family loyalty oath, and the most important commandment we lived with.

The strange thing about alcoholism in a family, is that in reality it only consumes about 30% of the alcoholic's life. But, the damage done to the family can be for a lifetime. In my Father's case he didn't start drinking heavily until after his mother died, shortly after my younger sister Kathy was born in 1952. And we all knew it and sensed a difference in the home. Our Mother played a strong role defining for us kids, the difficulties of Dad's important job at the bank. She stressed that we as kids must never get into trouble as it could negatively impact him and our family.

My big brother John, became our hero over the next few years, as he became our protector. Protector from our Father's "night terror", as we called it. It was our version of being woken up from a deep sleep and ordered downstairs for a chat with our Dad. He wanted us to know poetry, especially his favorite poets, and sing our favorite Irish songs together. We had to know philosophy and the great philosophers, but most important was knowing the history of our family. Rule number one was knowing how the McCarthy's came to this Country as Indentured Servants, a legal form of slavery. He told of how his Grandfather, a member of the IRB, was scheduled to be hanged in Dublin, for his fighting for Irish freedom, and how he escaped and came through Canada to be made a Postmaster in the Irish village of Tone, 4 miles outside of Pickford Michigan.

Of course we also had to box with him, he called it sparring. We couldn't be afraid to hit him, and he would just slap us boys. We had to be tough, he said. He would come home late, after community meetings, the Lion's Club and Kiwanis club, and an evening at the American Legion Hall, and sometimes the VFW Hall. The usual hour was a 3 o'clock in the morning wake up call. John would be taken downstairs from our bedroom to the kitchen. This was after we moved our family one block up Cedar St to a huge, 4 bedroom home, formerly owned by Otto Suppe, former Mayor of our town. It was Dad's time to teach his kids to be tough, and John, being the eldest, was the first Guinea pig, and he paid the price. John was a gentle boy, and very sensitive and caring. He was not one to be made tough., but he was brave. And he was the first among us to do so. There were many nights when Mom would tell us to just be careful and be very quiet, and not to alarm him, then she too would go downstairs, and try to get John back to bed.

There were a number of nights when John was facing Dad, when my sister Mary was so frightened she came into my bedroom and sat at the edge of my bed. We just talked and pretended not to be scared. I too was scared and we all were frightened, so I tried to get her to laugh and not really dwell on the craziness of this and let it go. We all went through the Jack McCarthy "night terror apprenticeship." Each of us at different times in our life. As I think back on it now, I'm glad I had John and Mary ahead of me, as when it became my turn for five years, I took a different approach.

We lived three different life's back then as kids, that helped us to survive. We had our family life, which can best be defined with tears, fears, laughter, and love. Then, our school life and extra curricular activities played a major role with us and our friends. Finally, for us boys, it was sports, basketball, football, hockey, and track. For my sisters, it was girl friends, participating in The Legion of Mary meetings after school, volunteering for the St Vincent DePaul Society, and helping the nuns. It wasn't until high school that dating, and having boyfriends and girlfriends had a positive change to our lives. That was our balance to the night terrors we were still experiencing. At least twice a week they occurred. We used to laugh at who was going to be the chosen one tonight, especially as John was getting older, and Mary and I knew we were next in line. It was always fun I thought when Dad would yell up and call upstairs to John and myself to come down to the kitchen. Mom wasn't pleased, but it didn't matter. John was very mindful of me, wanting to protect me, I was his little towhead brother and he took his role seriously. While I was always trying to get John to enjoy the event of our 3 am chat and laugh about this. That became my different approach. I wanted Dad to talk, tell us stories of the War, and his professional boxing career, sparring with Jack Dempsey, to recite the poetry he loved, his stories about sailing on the ocean and being on ship riding the thirty foot waves, and then we would read poetry he liked, and sing Irish songs we knew ourselves. One early morning John and I tried my plan with our Dad. We were reading the Robert Service poem, , 'The Rhyme of the Wage-slave', and we were acting out the Author's words by changing the tones of our voices. We both were having fun and laughing, while Dad was enjoying our presentation.

Excerpts From - 'The Rhyme of the Wage-Slave

When the long, long day is over, and the big boss gives me my pay,

I hope it won't be hellfire,

like some of the Parsons say,

and I hope it won't be hellfire

like some of the Parsons I've met,

all I want is peace and quiet,

a chance to rest and to forget.

Look at my brow toil furrowed,

look at me calloused hands,

Master, I've done thy bidding, wrought in thy many lands.

Wrought for the good master,

big bellied he be and rich.

I've done his desire for a daily hire, now I die like a dog in a ditch.

We both found out that night that our "night terror" didn't need to be fearful or frightening. Yes he could be mean, and frightening, and even unpredictable when he was drunk, and yes he was an alcoholic, but he had a special side to him. Once you tapped into that special side, you tapped into his soul. The closest person to him and knew him very well, was his older sister we called Doine. Our dear sweet Aunt. She told me several things I needed to know about my Dad, her younger brother. What made him special and what moved him. John and I just did what she said, And it worked. He could be very charming, and the evening was a lot of fun. But truthfully though, these fun times with enjoyment were few and far between. Everything wasn't "just peachy" or "rosey-dosey" as I said, my Father could be very unpredictable, so they were trial runs, and when it worked it was great. There were several nights too that mother would wake the three of us and we were shuffled off to Grandma's house, one block away so we could be safe, and out of his reach. Our baby sister Kathy stayed out of his reach most of the time, but she too suffered and felt the fear, as she was sharing a bedroom with Mary, in the big house. Going to our Gramas to spend our night was a horror show itself, but it was our "safe-house" and as I look back all four of us had what back then was called "a nervous stomach", a prelude to an ulcer which we all had as we grew into our teenage years. So cause and effect was certainly in play with all of us. But we managed to get up the next day, and off to school we went. We all entered into our other life for the day. Our family loyalty oath was still in effect, and it followed all of us through Grade School and High School. For me, it was my own personal problems I had with higher authority which the nuns represented very well, that became my challenge. And I became theirs in the third grade. And this was how Alcoholism in a family impacts everyone.

Thanks Pop

Another major force that kept family life somewhat under control, in addition to our Mother and Grama, was Pop, our Father's Dad. Just his presence kept things light and my brother and sisters turned to him for support, and he gave it. He moved in with us after my parents purchased the big house and he had his own bedroom. He lived with us until his death in 1959. He had a great sense of humor and with Dad going through his challenges, Pop filled a big family gap. He was a lumberjack, and was a sawyer by trade, and he and his brothers ran a saw mill near Pickford. Although he only went to the second book for his education, he was educated by the book of hard knocks, as he would say. He knew a lot about a lot of things, but a funny story I will always remember about Pop was this one. Dad and he used to take a car ride around "the horn" as they called it. It was a 28 mile circular trip down Pickford Road crossing over to Riverside Drive and back to the Soo. I was tucked into the back seat. It was a perfect trip on a Sunny weekend day for the two of them to drink a pint of scotch together, and have a family chat. Now Pickford road was a single lane gravel road as Pop remembered it. It had just been widened to a double lane road with a new slate of pavement and Dad wanted to show him the new Pickford road now called M-129. Pop was admiring the new paved highway and asked Dad, "Jack where are we, I thought you said we're going home to the old farm". My father told him we were, and got a great laugh out of that. Here was a man who came to the Soo with his family of 9 in a covered wagon up the old Mackinac Trail, but now on a modern highway, telling my Dad "Ah you've gone bugs Jack, this isn't the way home."

CHAPTER FIVE
Off to School

As I said earlier, we learned to live three different lives as children, and this helped us to survive the madness of Cedar Street. Now to be fair, my father's drinking was 2-3 days a week, and the night terror trips to the kitchen happened 1-2 times a week. So going to school was a happy time. Your friends were there and in my case after school we had hockey or football or basketball practice. This was the norm during my grade school years and from third grade on, I was a consistent visitor to the principal's office for improper behavior. My mother too was used to getting an office call to come and collect me after having a Parent-Teacher meeting. My mother was suspicious of my disrespect to the nuns as I just liked three of them, and certainly the principal of the School was the worst of them all. As I see it today, There was no question I was given a very good education, but that school was for John and Mary, not-myself. It was my Mother that wanted a Catholic education for her kids. Mary and John were the ones that enjoyed the school, I certainly didn't. So my first visit to a therapist was the decision of my mothers Parent-Teacher meeting. It occurred quite quickly and the focus was on my temperament and my feelings for authority. Nothing specific came from my three meetings with the therapist, as I recall, but my mother used that fact with the sisterhood, that I was getting emotionally repaired and my behavior would be changing. But not until my junior year in high school did therapy click in, and I made a major decision of my own as a result.

The third part of my life outside of family life, was dating and having someone special in my life that was important to me at that time. Who really knew at that young age of 16 what love was among boyfriend/girlfriend, But it certainly was special, and exciting and she was very kind and fun to be with. We shared a lot and got to know one another quite well. We did what young kids did, took off to see the latest movies, we went off to dances together, after school we went out for walks, at night we would chat on the phone for thirty minutes, we had fun. So my life was full, I had my sports and great friends, a sweet girlfriend, and a home life that still needed a close watch. So all of the McCarthy kids learned to live a life while the fear, anger, fright, love, and emotion were waiting for us at home on Cedar Street. At times it felt like we were walking on broken glass and that's how we were raised. It's a story of how alcoholism within a family is ruled by a loyalty oath. We had our own and we didn't violate it.

During high school, I had some great pals and friends, and we remained close throughout our University years, and some still to this day. We became great drinking friends too as we got into our early twenties. The funny thing about my friends and I, is our Father's all enjoyed the drink, and they all knew one another. Many were friends themselves from the American Legion, VFW connection or one of their favorite bars. Its impact on us was very deep, as it had a very special way of bonding us, as we all seemed to understand one another. Yes it's true, when we weren't fighting against other people we fought with ourselves. But we still remained deeply bonded.

Probably the greatest memory of my high school years in addition to our winning championships, was "Where were you when President Kennedy was assassinated?" It was November 22, 1963. I was a sophomore in our English class at Loretta, when over the public Address system came the horrible news that our President was shot and killed in Dallas. We were all in shock, who or why would someone do that? We of course felt it differently, I really believe. As he was our first Catholic President to get himself elected. It mattered back then, and it probably means very little today as Catholicism has become more mainstream, but we lived in a region where some of our local towns and villages looked down their noses if you were Catholic. We were called names, our priests were spit at, and were accused by some of the Protestant religions, as statue worshippers who believed in Roman rule. That helped promote bitterness, and hate, and stirred the ire of many Catholics. You can imagine how that incident promoted more drinking. And for the record, That's not an opinion that's a fact

But I never would have been able to get through High School without those bunch of guys and the teams we had, and my girlfriend at the time. It was during my Junior year that "the shit hit the fan," as my Dad would say.

As I started my junior year, it was to be the last year in the Old Loretto Catholic High School. A new school was being built and our class would be the first graduating class in the new school. Football season started in August and everyone was excited about continuing the winning season of the 1964 team that went undefeated and we won the bragging rights as Conference Champions. I had a starting position as outside linebacker and I was thrilled. I worked hard over the summer lifting weights and building muscle and adding speed with some extra weight. We finished the season with another winner and we were Conference Champions for the second year in a row. In the classroom, things were going well overall for grades, other than my failing Chemistry. I was warned by my Mother that if I failed I had to quit basketball and I had just made the varsity team. So although I still had a 2.5 grade point average, my Mother wanted to make a point of having me obey authority. I did as she asked but I dropped the chemistry class as quickly as I could. Or I should say I tried. I found that whole process interesting, as the school administration and the class teacher called my mother to ask me to stay in the class, and that I shouldn't worry as I will eventually get it with more time, referring to my chemistry class. Now that was the beginning of the war, they put their nose into my business and went so far as to get my own Mother to do their dirty work. We had another Parent-Teacher meeting with their team of three. I was livid, and I refused to go back to the chemistry class and told them, "they can fail me again if they choose." Well how this settled, was, I was to go to Catholic Social Services for once again more temperament therapy and I was to be suspended for three days from school for disrespecting authority. Going to the therapist kept me in high school, so weekly I went and visited Mr Calery. He was nice, enjoyed a laugh and I thought he was pretty cool. He was involved in the community so he knew my Father. Dad headed up the United Way Campaign which annually funded Catholic Social Services. So after 3-4 sessions the therapy sessions centered around my Father's drinking and the 'night terror' we experienced now into my teenage years. New therapy themes were being introduced during the 60's, and one was children of alcoholics. The professionals detailed the children's emotional baggage and impediments as they grew up. So now, I was a child of an Alcoholic and it was predicted I was to act in such a way, and react to challenges in a belligerent way. At my next visit I made my announcement to my Mother and to Mr Calery. I told him, "I refuse to be a child of an Alcoholic, and I refuse to take on their baggage," I will become an alcoholic myself if I have to, and create my own baggage. That's it and I walked out. My mother screamed and tried reasoning but it was falling to deaf ears. My Dad didn't hear about this until later on, as he was the president of the Loretto Athletic Association as well, and they were raising money for our school's sports teams. Beginning that day my relationship with my Father changed and at age 17, I began to drink with him at our 3 am visits. The school finally relented and chemistry was officially dropped, but to their surprise I graduated in the top third of my class. Yes, peace was declared my senior year, and our football team for the third year in a row were Conference Champions. I was headed off to our local College studying History and Political Science, something my Mother never thought I could achieve, but my father knew it all along. Years pass and forgiveness and acceptance becomes easier. Some of the greatest people in my world came out of that school, and for that I'm eternally grateful. I'm grateful to A very special Nun who saw in reading class I was in the slow readers circle with poor comprehension. But after she read aloud to the class, and asked questions, I was always the first to raise my hand with an answer. She discovered I was an Auditory learner and what I heard I memorized. I could listen and I needed to read out loud so I could hear what I read. I know now, it was the Authority issue and how it was used and abused by those with it. I know also, it was a definite reaction to what was happening for years on Cedar Street. The therapists called it learned behavior.

CHAPTER SIX

The College Years

It was 1966, and I was In my freshman year at our local College, called Lake Superior State. The Nation had survived the Cuban Missile Crisis in 1962, as well as the tragic assassination of our first Catholic President in 1963, an Irish American, the Civil Rights movement was beginning to have a greater impact on our country's leaders, as Walter Cronkite, a very respected news anchor on his nightly television show was showing black people were being beaten by police, with clubs, and police dogs biting and attacking peaceful crowds of people marching for their rights. And all they were marching for seemed simple enough, they were seeking their right to vote.

The VietNam war was beginning to inflame and a few local Soo boys in 1965-66 had been killed in early Action. The troop escalation was just beginning to increase significantly in 1967, so off to the draft board all 18 year olds needed to register to fill the demands of our Country's Army. A lovely Irish woman by the name of Mrs. Deuman was the registrar of the draft Board at the time, and she got to know each and every registrant. Her son was killed in Korea, and she had little regard for cowardice. She was decent, honorable and well respected. She felt each citizen had a duty, and signing up for the draft was an obligation of our citizenship. The Sault and region only had a few draft dodgers, and they left for Canada to avoid the draft. There were hundreds of Soo boys and those throughout our three counties, who were drafted between 1967-1969, and a number were seriously injured. Everyone lost one or two close friends killed in action. Upon returning back home, the stories of horror from that war became well known, and talked openly about. Protests with the local University became an annoyance to most of the public. We in the community did very little to honor our boys and many were our friends who returned home, no parades, no thanks, nothing! And I believe to this day, that was our shame, simply poor leadership. Those were our boys from the Sault, from Pickford, from Brimley, from Rudyard, from St Ignace and from Newberry who were getting shot at, or stepping on mines. They didn't start any war and were being patriotic and loyal to our Country, while being blamed for the war when they came home. It was our elected leaders who messed up, not our boys. And to some extent we have been paying for their mistakes ever since. Some came home crippled, others severely wounded, some were maimed, and many others had PTSD. There were more than a few of the boys who were exposed to Agent Orange, who suffered and died many years after the war ended. Being drafted was a two year commitment versus a regular Four year commitment of service to another branch of the military. I went down on my 18th birthday, and signed up, told them I was a full time student enrolled at Lake Superior. I was given a II-S deferment as a full time student. But once that status changed, or I dropped out of school, or kicked out of school because of poor grades, I needed to notify them. I would be given I-A status, which meant you were ready for draft physical and then active duty. So That's how 3 years of school went, the draft board, college exams, hanging out with friends and playing city league basketball, being with my girlfriend although I felt change was coming, and my father still "Holding Court.". In 1969 a draft lottery was coming, as the draft system had proven to be discriminatory. I gave up my ROTC 1-D military deferment. I was listed immediately I-A and ordered to go to Detroit's Fort Wayne, for my Military Physical. I was still in school full time but the military were needing numbers. Although I was listed I-A and passed my physical, I was not drafted as the lottery put a 90 day hold on future draftees by the old system. The lottery was deemed more fair as it was solely based on one's birthdate. Not one's social or economic status. It didn't care if you were going to school or not, once they drew your number you were called. Every three months they would draw numbers and dates. That first year of the lottery, my number was 241, and they drew up to 219 that year. Going into my final year as a senior, I no longer had to worry about the draft and I could finish school.

But 1969-1970, was my final year at Lake Superior State, and it was a miracle I got through it. I turned 21 in October, and I celebrated my birthday every day throughout the entire year. One of the major embarrassments I faced back then, was getting thrown in jail on my birthday, and arrested for disorderly conduct. The embarrassing part though was the bar fight I got in and having five stitches put in my cut eyelid and wearing a black eye, at least the other guy had a broken tooth. Disorderly conduct was a kind and polite way to say I was an unruly drunk. But, appearing before the judge it was a $40 fine, and he cared very little for my drunken behavior. He was the same judge I appeared three more times, over the next three years, and he was disgusted with me, the last time I was arrested. To prove it, he would only let my mother bail me out of jail, and not my father. Now think of that for a moment. My mother, who was trying her best to get her second son to respect authority, was the only person the judge would allow to get me out of jail. When she saw me, they unlocked the drunk tank door. I felt horrible that only she could claim me, and when she spoke, she said, "Get your chin up, and walk out of here like a man, don't let them see you with tears." My reaction was Wow, my mother finally had my back, and it felt good. It was an interesting development that came to light after the bail out event. My mother didn't say a word on the drive home, and I was waiting for a scolding. She just gave me a poem.

It was called, 'Your Name,

You got it from your Father,

Twas all he had to give,

So it's yours to use and cherish,

As long as you may live.

When you lose the gold watch he gave you,

It can easily be replaced,

But an ink spot on your name son,

Can never be erased.

It was spotless the day you took it,

A worthy name to wear,

When he got it, from his Father,

There was no dishonor there.

So it's yours, guard it wisely,

For when all is said and done,

You'll be glad your name is spotless,

When you give it to your son.

I've never forgotten that day, nor have I forgotten the look on her face. From that day forward until I went into the detox unit she spoke to me through poetry. She believed as our father taught us, all poetry has a special message. And maybe I could better understand the poet instead of listening to her. I have to compliment her as she never quit trying to find a way to communicate with me. Love comes in many forms, and several ways. She never quit! It just takes a sober mind to see it.

But, there was good news, playing basketball with our group of former Loretto grads, we won for the second year in a row, our City League ——-Men's Basketball tournament. We were champions again. The beginning of my Junior year my girlfriend and I ran out of gas and our relationship ended. So my senior year, there was more time to party and have fun, dating became fun again, and I made a little time for study. Our gathering place was the greatest bar ever, Hallesy's Bar. We all knew the owners and the Hallesy family, a great Soo Irish family, was known throughout the whole town. In fact, we went to school with the owner's children. As the tv series portrayed in its weekly show called CHEERS, Hallesy's had to be its model. It was a great little pub, with some of the greatest characters ever. Men of all ages, couples out to enjoy an evening of cards or cribbage, folks of every career, blue collar and white collar. It seemed like we all knew one another. Everyone was welcome. God how I loved that place. Now remember, and don't forget, I was just 21, and many of the older folks in the place were hard core drinkers. But we were used to that. In a few more years, I too at a young age would become a hard core drinker. And soon, the owner would ban me from the place, and no longer was I welcome there.

Getting ready for Graduation

My senior year at Lake Superior State was filled with excitement with my friends, craziness with my friends, and lots of Hallesy's Bar with my friends. My father's "Holding Court" for me was finally over, and now my younger sister and brother had to take their turn. I think I had an impact on Dad as I was still living at home. He changed some of his approach, and I felt bad that my little brother Tim, now 8, had to experience this "night terror". He had to face it on his own, as my younger sister who helped raise him and protected him, met an airman in our military and became engaged and married. There were so many nights when I came home after a night of drinking, I met my mother at the door. You could see hurt, disgust, and surrender in her eyes. All she would say is "I saved your dinner in the fridge, warm it up and get some food in you, I'm going to bed."

Everything at school my final year was adding up your earned credits to make certain you have the right number to graduate. All throughout my Junior year I was constantly on the Dean's list, and in the first quarter of my senior year I succeeded in getting good grades of 3.0 and above. I knew that I needed 28 more credits to graduate. But, I knew I wanted to have some fun, as this was supposed to be my last year of schooling. Which of course it wasn't. I was going through schools well into my 50's. So I decided on taking 14 credits per quarter and that would give me 186 credits on the nose, for my degree. I thought I could do that number in my sleep as I normally would take 16 credits per quarter. There were a number of times I would stop into Hallesy's and have a few pints and walk up the hill to the College to take my exam.

The Tale of Two Mindy's

One of my oldest and dearest friends in life, and still is to this day, came from a French family much like my mothers. So she thought he was walking on water. She just loved him. We met in the first grade and he was the first to teach me to play basketball. And we played together from 4th grade through our early twenties when our team won the City League Championship. He was truly a character and OMG did we have some fun. He was never one for trouble or for fighting. But he was game for almost anything, and never shied away from confrontation. In our time we were asked to leave two wedding receptions, we rolled a new vehicle twice and we were not injured, after the bars closed, we visited our local blind pig several times, we ran with the pack of friends sharing our limited funds, and covering our backs from trouble. But the time that he and I played house with the two Mindy's, had to be the very best of times. We laughed, roared and laughed some more.

The Two Mindy's were two lovely single girls, and quite pretty, with the same name and we referred to them both as Mindy. We met them every evening at a nightclub in town. We met in the early spring of 1970, about 3-4 months before my graduation. They were funny, great on the eyes, loved to chat and laugh, and dance, and yes, one other thing. Both of these beautiful girls were engaged. But they also enjoyed their drink too, so we both thought it was a perfect match. Let's have some fun, and boy did we ever.

Graduation and the Great Party, off to jail once more

Well I graduated , and I was happy to finish and walk down the aisle at the Pullar Stadium, in June where the graduating class of 1970 took place and received my BA in History and Political Science. Pp My parents were thrilled, and my Mother most especially. It was they that suggested we have one of My Mothers prime rib dinners, and celebrated with a McCarthy party. Every guest who was invited was asked to bring bottles of Bush-mills Irish whiskey, Cutty Sark Scotch Whiskey, Jim Beam or a six pack, and my mother would feed them up with fried chicken and roast beef, roasted and mashed potatoes, corn on the cob, two salads, with pies and a large cake with ice cream. It was my Parents who wanted to throw a nice party for me, my friends, and family. My Father bought the keg, and Mother cooked the meal, and we celebrated. What a great meal and what a party. It was a fun-filled party, and everyone was happy. The meal was tremendous and mom really went out of her way to do it up right. God loves her. My friends, for my graduation gift, arranged for me to have a date with one of the Mindy girls I was seeing, and get together later that night at our-nightclub, to continue the celebration. So it was going to be a great evening. There was music and laughter everywhere, we heard the Clancy Brothers, and the Dubliner's but there was a Song by the Irish Rovers we played at the party and the song's message all came true. So while we were laughing and singing, the truth of that evening slowly developed.

'Wasn't That a Party'

Could have been the whiskey, might have been the gin.

Could have been three or four six-packs,

I don't know, but look at the mess I'm in,

My head is like a football, I think I'm gonna die,

Tell me, me oh me oh my,

Wasn't that a party?

Someone took a grapefruit and wore it like a hat,

I saw someone under my kitchen table, talking to my old tom cat,

They were talking about hockey and the cat was talkin' back,

Along about then everything went black,

But wasn't that a party?

I'm sure it's just my memory playin' tricks on me,

But I think I saw my buddy cuttin' down my neighbour's tree,

My head is like a football, I think

I'm going to die,

Tell me, me oh me oh my wasn't that a party.

Well after about 4-5 hours at the McCarthy party thanking everyone for attending and sharing their gifts and congratulating me, off we all went to Hallesy's bar. My brother John joined us too and we played cribbage, and had our pool table challenge. John and I were partners. He was always the better cribbage player, but I had the better pool stick. So, when 9-10 pm came, off we drove to the Northview nightclub, but first a stop at the Belvedere Ships Lounge, another nightclub. Well you can imagine after 7 hours of drinking and having fun, something was going to happen. And by 11pm we landed at the Northview to go dancing and continue to celebrate.

Everything was joyous and everyone was in good form, it's great we had my Mother's dinner, but then an argument started at the bar with my brother John in the middle of it. I ran up to make sure he knew I had his back as four brave men circled him. John was never one to punch anyone, he would just throw bodies aside or over the bar. And John was the strongest man I had ever known. Really, John didn't need my help at all, as I was jarred myself. But he was my big brother with a young son. That's all I needed and I hit the biggest fella there when the others jumped on me. John reacted like you would expect, I was his little brother and he was my protector growing up. He never punched anyone but bodies were thrown everywhere, just like they were bags of 50 pounds of potatoes. Pat, the owner, called the police and they came immediately. As things were calming down he told them to take John McCarthy, "that big guy", as the guy who caused the trouble. But the whole point was, they were to pick up John McCarthy.

Everyone was calming down, and were getting back to normal and celebrating. I was sitting back at our table, When the police came up to us and said, " McCarthy, you're coming with us, you're under arrest," You see for the third time, the same policeman who arrested me at 18, for fighting, at my 21st birthday for drunken disorderly conduct and now after my college graduation, did so again. He knew I was a McCarthy and so I was arrested, but this time my name was John McCarthy. I went with them very respectfully, and peacefully, not disorderly and it's surprising how quickly you can sober up. I kept telling them, they arrested the wrong person and my name is not John it's Mike, and the arresting officer knew damn well that to be a fact. I asked them throughout "what am I being arrested for and being charged with"? They responded and said "Drunk and disorderly." But, their cold response I thought was, "we will let the judge figure that out." I was brought to the jailhouse, and walked down in handcuffs to their drunk tank and spent a good 3 hours there. The alcohol I consumed then took over and I really became drunk. My friends raised the bail money and off I went to one of their homes and fell asleep. I woke up by noon, and my God the stories began. So I spent my graduation night in a drunk tank. Yes, the party was great, but instead of being with one of the Mindy girls, I was once again in jail, drunk. But on Tuesday morning the following week, I was ready to go see the judge and face the charge in court. The judge who knew me, saw me sitting down in the courtroom, and I said to him, "Good morning judge". He said "good morning," and asked "McCarthy, what are you doing here?" His clerk said, "He is on the docket this morning, your Honor." His comment really got to me, and it was really the first of three Dominoes of my drinking life to fall, he said, "For God's sake man, why don't you just quit drinking." His words went right through me, and made me sick. I surrendered my bail money as the fine and kept my mouth shut on the arrest itself. I knew after my court appearance, change was coming, but what I didn't know was how fast.

CHAPTER SEVEN

Joining the Merchant Marine

I spent the early weeks of that summer of 1970, after my graduation , at the University working with their youth development summer program, called Upward Bound. My dear family friend Pam told me about it and thought it would be a good match after my graduation. The youth came from all parts of the Region of three Counties. It was a very good program and the young teenage kids had a great learning experience. The program's aim and goal was to have the youth continue on their education and not drop out of school. Their success numbers were things to brag about. It was working. Kids were getting scholarships to move onto College, and some went to serve our Country in the military. But to everyone's delight, not one single student tied to the program's Outreach effort dropped out of school.

So after that 6 week gig ended, I immediately went down to our U.S. Supply Company, an affiliate of the U.S. Steel company and signed up to join the Merchant Marine and spend the rest of the Summer, Fall and early Winter on ship working on the oar boats. If you could do the work, there was good money to be made. A good friend from high school Jon worked there and he took my application and whatever he did, he processed it immediately and within a week he called me and told me "You have a ship. It will be in Cedarville at their quarry. The ship is called the Henry M Crawford, but it's an Inland Steel ship, not a U.S. Steel ship." Not that it matters, but "you will have to go to the Coast Guard Base in St Ignace and take the Merchant Marine Oath from Commander Sperry, and he will swear you in." So my father drove me down to St. Ignace from the Soo, with a packed bag of clothing to take My Oath to serve. Now understand this formality - An oath may be administered by any Coast Guard-designated individual or any person legally permitted to administer oaths in the jurisdiction where the person taking the oath resides. And here was my oath I took in September of 1970. With my Father holding the Bible and my left hand on it with my right hand raised. I repeated Commander Sperry and his words, I do solemnly swear or affirm that I will faithfully and honestly, according to my best skill and judgment, and without concealment and reservation, perform all the duties required of me by the laws of the United States. I will faithfully and honestly carry out the lawful orders of my superior officers aboard a vessel.

I finished the Oath and shook the commander's hand, and his response was perfect. "Congratulations, Mike, you're now married to the ship."

So off we drove to Cedarville and I said goodbye to Dad. I boarded the ship at 7 p.m. on a windy, rainy night, with a scheduled time to exit the port by 11 pm that evening.

I was met by the first mate who took me aboard and brought me immediately to the Engine room and introduced me to the Chief. We all called him with respect, Chief. I was assigned there, as a coal passer was needed to work the coal furnaces. The ship Henry Crawford was one of the last Coal Ships on The Great Lakes. A 550 foot ship who carried its coal right on top deck, and funneled it down to the engine room and its furnaces. We weren't one of the new self unloaded ships, so we needed Port assistance more than the newer ships did, but we carried tons of ore from the mines to the mills.

It was time for my training and orientation as my shift was starting right at 11 pm just as the ship was pulling back from its docking. The Chief took me aside and explained my role as Coal Passer and assistant Fireman, and we toured the Engine room and he pointed out different aspects of what makes things work, and by the way he said, "Mac, you're going to take the bells too." From that point on I was called Mac, as that was how the engine room operated. We had nicknames for everyone who worked there. The most important people I worked with were the firemen. They were the ones who filled the furnaces with coal, while I pulled out the clinkers as they were called, which was how coal burned and created heat thru coagulation. So we emptied the furnaces and they filled them. Then we watered them down, ground them up and pushed them through the ship's vacuum, which blew the clinkers and dust into the Lake we were sailing in. The next person of importance was the Chief, who always was there to take the commands coming into Port. The assistant chief would work the engines out on the lake but very rarely did we keep the bells until we were heading to park the ship. My job was to record and register the bells, which rang out upon receiving commands from the captain in the front of the ship. It worked like a telegraph system like the old Western Union offices in our Country. I had a short time requirement to register the command and then the engine room and chief could respond . I pressed the bell button and registered the command and the Chief acted accordingly.

The next tour of my area was to check out my sleeping arrangements with the other coal passers who I shared the room with. It's there I met Eddie, and Tony C. Their nicknames were of interest. You see we had a ship roster of 28 men, but needed at least 3 more to fill out what was needed. 24 of the 28 men on the ship were of Finnish descent. All from the Iron Range region of Minnesota, Wisconsin and the Upper Peninsula of Michigan. And although they were very friendly to work with, courteous and helpful, they never spoke to us in English when we weren't working together. They were very clannish.

The nicknames they gave us were funny but interesting how they came up with them. We had Eddie, an American Indian from the L'Anse-Baraga region of the Upper Peninsula, and he was of the Ottawa tribe, so he was called Tonto. Apparently Tonto of the Lone Ranger fame was in fact an Ottawa Indian. Eddie was my roommate and a coal passer too, he was very quiet, but kind until he went into Port and had a few drinks at a local bar. Tony C the other coal passer was an Italian kid from Duluth, Minnesota where half the Finns on our ship came from. They knew of Tony's family and their business, so it was appropriate they felt he be called and known as Don Antonio. It didn't seem to bother him and he just laughed it off. As I said earlier I was simply called Mac. Now we had the chief Steward on the ship, a big man by the name of Johnny Q. He too came from the Hibbing/Duluth region as his father came to Minnesota as a Mining Engineer from Belfast, Northern Ireland. He knew many of the Finn's also and simply didn't like them at all. But Johnny could cook and handle the kitchen, and was loved by all the officer's on the ship, and the chief engineer and his assistant loved him. Now these men too were again Finnish, but they were smart, and although they participated with all their Finnish friends and spoke Finn, they understood the value of building a team on the ship and many of them went to the Merchant Marine Academy. Johnny Q. was called Big John, a name which he enjoyed. So the four of us talked with each other all the time and when the ship was at Port we all would walk to the nearest bar or we all took a cab to get there. But we always hung out.

They were fun times watching Johnny Q at breakfast and dinner talking to the Finn's while serving them. The officers are always before the rest of us and loved Johnny's meals, and they didn't mind one bit the arguing the sailors would have with their Chief steward. We three Coal passers really enjoyed how he ridiculed them, taunted them, and teased them, and told them unless they speak English he will burn their food he prepared for them. It made things light for us, and we all enjoyed each other's company on the ship and off. But it was at a Port town in Ohio, and Illinois, and even in New York the four of us had the greatest fun. All four of us loved a good jar of draft beer. We all had to be careful because we were off the ship and couldn't show back to work drunk. Now that worked well for us Coal Passers but not our head Cook. He loved having for his drink a shot of bar whisky and a beer chaser. The other thing about Johnny Q., was he was a boxer, as was Eddie. And the more they drank, the more they wanted to see if they both still had it. Tony C and myself became the good guys for a change and kept our mates out of trouble. That seemed to work well as we were limited with our time off the ship, as we were working 4's and 8's, or four hours on, with eight hours off. We followed that routine several times as we went out on a port city. In his kitchen, Johnny Q started to really like us three, and did his best to serve us prime everything for our meals, while he intentionally burned the food of the other shipmates. They, being just as stubborn, still refused to speak English to him, but they made the mistake of complaining to the ship's officers of how poorly Johnnie was feeding them. That was a big mistake and it backfired as the officers who loved their chief cook, lectured us all about ships' respect for higher authority and Johnny being the chief Steward and head cook with 20 years of experience deserve our respect and support. The Finns were allowed to be clannish in a port city but not on ship. A definite win for Johnny and how he enjoyed it.

The whole experience of being in the Merchant Marine was fun and interesting. But the money was good. Especially when Tony C checked out at the end of September. That left Eddie and Myself, now working 6 on 6 off. So 12 hours a day and as I said the money became really great. My drinking stopped somewhat, at least it was drastically reduced. It did really until the infamous Lorraine wedding party in October. Johnny Q had been on the ships for twenty years and in that time had met hundreds of people. Well an old girl friend from Lorraine, Ohio invited him to a wedding of a mutual friend they knew. Johnnie jumped at the chance to see his old girlfriend again and invited Eddie and Myself to join him. Now, It's very rare your ship stays docked after they drop their load and go to pick up another, but this time we would be at our port city for 2 days and we had to budget our time to enjoy our upcoming wedding reception and put in the time for your shift back on the ship. We were determined to take care of business and show up and have fun at a wedding reception. We would even buy a suit and go show some class there in Lorraine. That was all fine and dandy and we were having a great time, until an argument broke out with of course Johnny Q right in its center. Now Johnny was 6' 5" In height, a boxer, and ready and waiting for the worst to happen. Eddie immediately jumped in and began to challenge those who were arguing with Johnnie. I really thought for a moment I was back home in the Soo with my friends ready for the row. I just wanted to have a few drinks, but there we were and the fight broke out. And I really don't know if it was Johnny or Eddie who threw the first punch, but they were fun to watch. I didn't do much really, but I did pick up a stool and cracked a few people over the head, trying to jump on my friends and I did manage to kick a few too. I wish it would have been filmed seriously as watching Johnnie and Eddie standing and punching anyone who crossed their path was something right out of an old John Wayne movie. Then what often happens in a brawl, someone violates the rules of a bar fight, and breaks a bottle of beer over Johnnie's head and cuts him pretty badly behind his right ear. Eddie was doing good too until 5 people jumped on him and started to beat on him. I jumped on the guy with the broken beer bottle and knocked it out of his hand and we wrestled and punched one another, until the police came.

It was a true Soap Opera. Johnnie's date was quite angry, of course, until she found out he needed 12 stitches in his head. Eddie was smiling and quite happy with himself, with his two front teeth knocked out. I too needed 3 stitches as I was punched with my glasses on and they cut me below my right eye on my cheekbone, Now that was just us, the couple who were married were disgusted, and then they found out, it was their friends who argued with Johnnie, and Eddie, and admitted they threw the first punch. The best part was they were beaten up pretty badly. The Married couple were very embarrassed, as we were outnumbered twelve to three. So the police asked us to head back to the ship, and in fact offered to give us a ride, but we refused but we thanked them. The wedding reception continued, and no charges were made or sought. Everything was dismissed. Johnny and I went to get stitched up at the Emergency ward, and Johnny and his old girlfriend made up for his next trip into Lorraine. That was some night.

The Bells Put To Use

Two months passed since our fiasco in Lorraine, and we pals now the three of us, became very close friends. Even our meals were more friendly as the clannish Finns appreciated and respected the new rules, and they were happy to be a shipmate and talk openly in English. No one cared what they did while we were at Port city. Even Johnny enjoyed serving everyone, and as he healed up and had his stitches removed, he was ready to go again. Eddie at our next stop in Cleveland right after our 2 day stay in Lorraine, went to see a Dental specialist and had fitted a front plate of new teeth. But he was still happy. So the time was closing in on us, we had two maybe three more trips at most before the shipping season closed for the year. It was early December and we were headed once again for Lorain, Ohio. I was assigned to the bells in the Engine Room, that I previously defined my duty and the chief was right beside me. Now Black River of Lorraine, Ohio has several bends and tight turns going to their Steel Mill, and a very slow speed is required. Several hundreds of ships were built there in their history, and the river was very user friendly for a 550 foot ship.

Now the chief Engineer had sailed in and out of Lorraine several times over 25 years and was suspicious from the beginning as we entered into the river from Lake Erie when the call came down for slow ahead. The chief immediately said "Mac, get this down and ring back." Here is what the Captain can order. Many ships have the following dial or bell instructions: Full ahead, half ahead, slow ahead, dead slow ahead, stop, dead slow astern, slow astern, half astern, and full astern. He was thinking dead slow ahead first. About 10 minutes later, moving slowly ahead, the order came down full ahead. Now remember I said there are many bends in the river, well immediately the chief yelled, "Get that fuckin order recorded Mac, ring the bell and close it. "Then hang on, we're going to hit something." Then sure enough 3 minutes later the ship hit ground and we drove our Crawford ship through a dock and onto the ground. The chief told me to secure the bells and don't run out until I took care of that first. We had four floors to walk up. We were taking in water in the rear of the ship where we were in the Engine room. Fortunately, the ship's pumps were working. So there you have it, what a mess. A large Coast guard enquiry was held for three days, and I was called in to show the bells had not been tampered with and were secured. And they were. The unfortunate part was the Coast guard took the license of the Captain and his first mate who had been drinking. Their orders were followed, and the bells had proven their stupid order took place. The chief engineer was honored for his professionalism. The chief said to me, quietly, "Thanks Mac."

All I could think of, as I was a nervous wreck, was the ship was going to sink. That wasn't going to happen in reality, but I never thought for one minute that the Captain and his First mate were drinking on the job. At no time did I think of those damn fools doing that, we all knew the rules. The Chief sure did.

Over the next three days water was being pumped out and ship welders were flown in to repair the ship the best they could. They finished and most of the damage was fixed but a hole was still there in the stern of the Ship. The final order came down from the Coast Guard to take the ship back up to its Port in Duluth. The Company flew into Lorraine, a new executive team, to take the ship on its final trip of the year back to Duluth. Our order was to lay the ship up there, and get the ship into dry dock. Now that meant sail the ship over Lake Huron, then over Lake Superior with a hole still in its stern. And to do that in the month of December. Anyone who ever sailed the lakes in winter would never take a broken ship out into Lake Huron and forget Lake Superior, it won't happen! Well it did and the company of Inland Steel paid a handsome premium to everyone who sailed the ship back to Duluth. I was one, and everyone else who stayed were nervous, but were nicely paid. Eddie said goodbye, he wasn't going to lose his life like that and passed up on his season's bonus and left. It was hard to say goodbye but we gathered in the kitchen and watched Johnnie serve up some Apple pie with ice cream. Then he left, he was a great guy.

But we did sail it, and not even a wave in either Lake did we face. We couldn't move at top speed, So Half ahead was the fastest we could go. It was a long trip back to Duluth, it took us 6 days. We landed at our Port, and docked our ship for repair. I spent another two days on the ship. I then took my pay which was wonderful. I said goodbye to Johnnie, and we went into Duluth for a goodbye drink. The ship owners gave me some travel money to get my Greyhound Bus ticket to get back home to the Soo. I checked into a hotel for the night, got my bus ticket, got some dinner, and took a taxi to a sailors bar we always visited when we hit Port. I stayed there until the bar closed and took a taxi back to my hotel. I awoke at 9 am and left for the nearby Greyhound Station for my 9 hour bus trip back home, on December 20, 1970.

CHAPTER EIGHT

My Development Career Begins

When I returned back to the Soo after my adventure on the Inland Steel Ship the Crawford, my Dad made a few calls to business friends and set up an interview for me with a regional development program in our three rural counties called Community Action. They were based in the Sault with offices throughout our Region. It was part of the Office of Economic Opportunity, a National program to fight and reduce poverty and create employment for people with lower incomes. Our region in the Upper Peninsula of Michigan had a very high percentage of poverty and high unemployment during the fall and winter months. My Father knew the director pretty well and he knew also the Chairman of their Board, and both men agreed to meet me between Christmas and New Year in 1970. This was to be my first professional job and the fact I had my degree I qualified for consideration. So I was ready to begin my new life on a professional scale, I just needed to be at my best with the interview, my very best. I thought the interview went well with both men, and I enjoyed meeting both of them. Gordon was the Director of the CAA and former Superintendent of one of our region's school systems. Ron was the Chairman of Community Action and he was the Director with another local social service body committed to the cause of reducing poverty and unemployment of the lower income population of our region. I thought they were both solid men and deeply believed in what they were doing. So I was happy to get a phone call early on New Years Eve that I should come into work on January 3rd and begin. I was elated, but not thinking or knowing that making more money for me, really meant spending more money for drinking. I can't believe I'm saying this but it was true. How stupid could you get but the addiction had already set its teeth into me. and I was on the alcohol waterwheel and with each drink the wheel moved faster, and over time, I was unable to get off.

During my time at CAA I worked with and met some of the finest people in my hometown. I had a great first year and my annual review was top notch. My drinking was mainly on weekends, and I kept my public life separate from my private life. The man who hired me and was my boss for that first year was Gordon, and he left and moved back into his first love of Education. Ron, who was the chairman, became the Executive Director, and things changed and we really grew the organization. He immediately promoted me to be his Deputy Executive Director and gave me free rein to develop programs and write for grants that would help us meet our mission. He was a big picture guy who worked with the politicians regardless of party and new program areas of employment and training, transportation, housing, energy assistance, and senior citizens meals, all emerged and gave the organization political clout it never had. By mid year of 1972 we tripled the budget and we were adding new people to the organization. People in our community and our Elected leaders started to see the CAA as a vehicle to their success, and Ron knew how to play that game as previously he too was an elected party politician.

But slowly my personal life was interfering with my public image. Success breeds success as they say, well that applies to the drink as well. The more success we had the more I drank after each work day, and into the night. Part of my job was to involve myself with various community based non profits and I did. So at least three times per week I was at a community organization meeting and when they finished I would head straight to the bar and meet up with some of the boys or I would be joined by a board member for a casual drink and some comradery.

Although I was getting high grades for my work and securing significant amounts of work in money from grant funds for our programs, I had started to show up to work not just hungover but still drunk from late nights. Much like my Father and his 3 am wake up calls. I was approached by three people whom I liked a great deal, who worked with me. They confronted me about my drinking. They too knew alcoholism as I did, but I never was asked the bottom line question before, "Do you have a drinking problem Mike? Can we help you in any way?" So I did what the best of us do, I started to call in sick to avoid the embarrassment of being called out and held accountable. There was a lot of flu going on with me, at least twice a week, when eventually Ron called me into his office. Ron was far from being perfect himself, and drank himself sometimes to excess, but he was the boss, and believed enough in me to give me time to clean myself up. It wasn't until a month or so later he held a party at his house with several people, including board members, and local leaders with several politicians. I got into a heated argument with one of our local politicians that Ron was trying to court. He had been drinking just as much as I, and I really should have known better, but we argued over employment training for older Americans that I had researched the need and the numbers were horribly tilted against people 55 and above. He argued back and said most of them were just lazy. So I scolded him, and threatened to run against him and told him how I was going to defeat him. I called him a few rude names, and Ron got upset and came in to calm things down. He asked me to leave and I did. But first I told Ron he would be an idiot to back this guy and shame on him for taking his side. Then I left. So on Monday morning, the very first thing Ron called me into his office. It was not a friendly conversation as he was put out, and still angry with me, that I did what I did. He simply gave me an ultimatum, that I get help now or I leave the organization. He knew I had a drinking problem, and told me so, and that I better wake up and admit it, or my life will be ruined. "Don't be foolish, get some help, and do it now." Well, that was the second domino to fall and my time was narrowing before my crash at my parents house on Christmas.

CHAPTER NINE

The Dominoes have all Fallen

From June 1, through December 24th, those 215 days will always be remembered for three reasons. The First, was my health was deteriorating quickly, I came down with two separate ulcers, I was passing blood in my urine, and I had the shakes so bad that without a shot of vodka every morning, and one in the afternoon, I had a hard time getting a 24 year old body and brain to move, the Second, the alcohol waterwheel was moving at top speed with my daily intake of booze now at four six packs of beer a day. I was eating very little, so of course the ulcers were finding a way to cause its damage, and Third, my worst offense, I was arrested for the fourth time by the same police officer from my 3 previous bouts with the law, but my offense this time was being charged with Drunk Driving. I lost control of my car, sliding on ice, in late October of 1972, and hit a fire hydrant and then boomeranged through an older couple's front porch and steps. All on Ashmun Street in the Soo.

Yes I was drunk, and at fault, and felt horrible that I lost control of my car and hit the porch of that lovely elderly couple. Two policemen came to the scene and when I saw it was the same policeman, I said something smart and of course rude, but he made a mistake and clubbed me over the head with his flashlight. His partner that night was one of the Rotary Saints of the East End, our Police Family. He didn't appreciate the physical force used by his partner and jumped between us. He asked first, if I was injured by the accident. I told him no, but as the old saying goes, the strangest turn of the whole concern was only just beginning, because of the hard bang to the head, it created about an hour of me being sober, Perfectly sober! They didn't have a breathalyzer test in their car so they had me do the alcohol road tests of walking with your eyes closed, going frontwards and backwards, and balancing yourself holding one leg behind your back. I passed them with flying colors much to the arresting officers' chagrin.

The kind officer wanted to charge me with reckless driving, but at a minimum they needed to book me in jail because of public property damage, and most important was the private property damage I was responsible for. They put me in a heated cell for an hour and by the time I got out, I was a slobbering drunk. It was then they gave me a breathalyzer test and I blew .27. I was booked in, finger printed, had a mugshot, and I went right to the drunk tank, and as I said earlier My dear Mother was the only one who could bail me out. This was ordered by the Judge who had his fill of me.

There was a great legal fight that took place. The arresting officer wanted to get a minimum sentence of 30 days to 90 days in Jail and a DUI conviction with the loss of my drivers license. But his partner the Rotary Saint was more flexible and wouldn't agree, and I know he had his father Lt. Al to call me and told me to get in touch with the private home owners immediately. I went to visit the older couple right away, not only to apologize but to truly show how sorry I was. They were a lovely Italian couple who had a business in their house, and they knew my Father from the bank, and their son went to school with my brother John, and they knew and liked John very much. The arresting Police Officer needed the couple to push his charges and it would have been a done deal, but they refused to press charges and he was left out in the cold. I did have to agree to pay for damages, and agree to an Impaired driving charge, not a DUI, with a $500 fine. After it was over I went back to visit with the couple and thanked them. And here is what that lovely Old Man said to me, "Son, do yourself and my wife a favor, please, quit drinking, you're killing yourself, and you don't even know it. So please quit." My eyes were filled with tears, and I thanked both of them. I didn't tell him, I just couldn't quit. That was the Third domino to fall, and from that point forward I was living on borrowed time. That alcohol water wheel was moving faster and faster. In two weeks I was heading to my parents for Christmas dinner. The timing for the collapse had arrived.

CHAPTER TEN

A Tribute to My Mother

A lot has been written about my Mother in this book. Her civility, her deep devotion to our Lord, and the Blessed Mother, her deep loyalty and love of family, and her three principles of faith, of hope, and of charity. I thought her mode of communication with me growing up was quite unique, and it worked. A poet once wrote of his own Mother that touched me deeply. As I read it, I thought he was writing about my own Mother. He wrote "We are born of love; Love is our mother. When you look into your mother's eyes, you know that is the purest love you can find on this earth." My Father who deeply loved his mother always said to me, "Your mother is the only one who can take the place of all others but whose place no one else can take." Life doesn't come with a manual, he would say, it comes with a mother.

Being married to a chronic alcoholic husband and for myself growing up with an alcoholic father, had to be hard on her too, as it was with my brothers and sisters. For the longest time, I didn't give that a moment of thought. It was all about me, not her. How shameful was that. I shared in this book her feelings on why she stayed and never left their marriage. But she never expressed how scared she had to be as well. She tried and tried in vain to get him away from us at 3 am and then she would take us to Grandma's house, where we could at least sleep before going to school. She then tried to calm him and was not too successful I'm thinking. I know at times I would be more angry with her and not him for an evening of terror. But as I said, it had to be hard on her, as she too succumbed to my Dad's behavior. In other words, to live with him, she drank with him. In doing so she became an alcoholic herself. Now that's twisted too isn't it? But that's the secret of an alcoholic family. Abuse is always a part of an alcoholic family. However, She found her way and fought her way back and came through it by turning her life over to our Lord. I guess I was more understanding of her than with my father, but I was angry with her, for being so foolish. And then, I became so proud of her for how she found her way out. We as Kids needed and wanted protection, but we learned how to survive on our own. The craziness was we actually thought we could understand the alcoholic more than our defender could. It's a terrible truth of family alcoholism. As times moved on, I came to peace with the horror of my youth. And as she taught us, I learned to Accept and Forgive. And as I sit and reflect on her complex self, her grace, her love for her family, and her quirky character, I can say warmly with love. I miss my Mother. The loss of your mother no matter how old you are, changes your life forever. Your mother is your forever friend. You never really get over the loss, but you learn to live with it. She is never far away from your thoughts. And She is always in your heart. For memories are all we have when I think of her today. Your name I will always honor Mum, I'm glad you passed my way. You are Always, In my heart.

CHAPTER ELEVEN

A Tribute to My Father

I've written a lot about the good, the bad and the ugly of my father, and he was all of that. You've read about my quoting the Irish playwright Sean O'Casey and his reference to the Irish people of being brilliant, beautiful and foolish. That too was a fair depiction of my father. But I think the best reference was taken from the Irish Author, Frank McCourt in his book Angela's Ashes, as he called his Irish father, his own Blessed Trinity. He was God, the good Father, the good Son, but the devil himself. And I've written in great detail at his worst, he left roads of scars in each of his children. His abuse of parental power led me down the path of being a total contrarian, and one not to be trustful of authority. I felt that's been abused and used improperly. Hence my dislike, and distrust for most Priests, Nuns and Police.

But my Father too was special, humorous, charming, great in debate, a man who loved poetry, with a brilliant mind, and a great social conscience with love for the underdog, and simply a lovely gentleman when he was sober. One of the great gifts of my family, no doubt given to us all by our Mother, was to Accept and Forgive. That became a hallmark of our family.

There is no doubt that if he were alive today, and I were to ask him, "what the hell were you thinking Dad, we were little kids, and you scared the hell out of us with your Drinking. Waking us up at 3 am to talk to us, telling us family stories, reciting poetry, singing Irish songs, yes, we did it, but you scared the hell out of us doing it. What were you thinking?" That question I have pondered for a long time, and I believe I found the answer today, now that I'm 75. He would say something like this. "I know I failed you Mike, and I know I hurt you, your brothers and sisters, and I do wish I could take it all back. I can't but I'm truly sorry. I wanted each of you to be yourselves, not something society wanted you to be, not being pigeonholed. But, what each of you wanted. I wanted each of you to be strong enough, and tough enough to stand up for yourself and stay true to what you wanted. You don't need to surrender to anyone, it's there you will find your happiness. That's what I wanted for you and your brothers and sisters to be happy and proud and independent." "I just couldn't say it sober, because of my own fear, and failure, and I'm sorry." As I said earlier, it makes the case doesn't it, for acceptance of who he was, and what he did, but without forgiveness, who are we and what are we?

My friends, Tim, Paul, Fred, Harrison, Dan, Jim, Phil, all enjoyed the charm and craziness of my Dad. And my Dad enjoyed chatting with all of them. They enjoyed his stories of his first girlfriend who lived up in Algonquin, and how her older sister loved flirting with him. He even wrote a poem about her. He would recite:

Here's to my girl who lives up on the hill,

If she won't kiss me, her sister will,

Here's to her sister.

And everyone would raise their glass to toast her sister.

Other stories they enjoyed were his sparring with former Boxing Champion Jack Dempsey during the war. They loved to hear of his three professional boxing matches in Soo Canada all with the same middleweight Tom Armstrong. His fishing stories were great about flying with Ontario bush pilots into Northern Canada lakes. One of the funniest was Dad frying up a 4 ounce tenderloin, slow frying it, so it was nice and juicy. My brother John came by and turned the heat up, to help cook the steak with Dad not knowing it. The heated frying pan burned the steak when Dad jumped up and got so angry he threw the frying pan through the kitchen door. These were great stories to share a pint and a six pack or more, and everyone loved it. He would drink his Scotch with milk to coat his stomach so his ulcers would not create problems for him. My friends loved that part of him, and would spend hours just carrying on with him.

I thank God I was in my sobriety program for several years seeing my Father finding his own sobriety. We had hours of chats and his insight was the most important part of building my career. It was even more beneficial as it was this time in life, He and My Mother fell in love all over again. I know he spent hours too with my older siblings, my brother John and my sister Mary. They too needed to see and feel the depth and heart of their Dad, and did.

I remember later after my Dad passed, my Mom and I were talking about him. And I asked Mom this, "Mom, you know how much I loved Dad and understood him the best I could, but I have to ask you, why on earth did you stay and live with that maniac when he was drinking, he was crazy and hurtful!" Her answer really defined the times for my mother, who she was and what she was. She said,"Dear I so loved the man, and knew he was so bright, and charming, I taught myself during those bad years, to close one eye, and not look at him with the other. When I grew up, you accepted things you don't accept today, and we made our own bed, and it was mine to lay in. And I did so, hoping the real man would come back to me. It was something I prayed for daily and kept hoping. It took most of our lifetime but look at him today. He came back to me." Once again a case for acceptance and forgiveness.

CHAPTER TWELVE

51 years of Sobriety, December 24, 2023

I retired at the age of 70. In that time frame of my 50 year working career, I travelled about 2.7 million air miles, and received life time status as a million miler with United Airlines and Delta Airlines. My travels have taken me around the world, meeting with CEO's and community leaders, Boards of Directors, Mayors, Governors, and an assortment of governmental leaders. I've worked in 37 of our 50 States. I'm very proud of our bottom line, my companies raised over $400 million in 119 capital campaigns throughout our Country and Canada, and thousands of jobs were created. We had a lot to do with seeing the Colorado Rockies start up in Denver, and the $2 million of seed money that we raised for the DIA airport was the critical first step to its development, and the Light rail in Denver was completed by our company team with our client the Denver Chamber of Commerce, and their EDC. Not that much of this really matters, but what I've learned in the process is worth sharing. It is a fact and not an opinion, that we do stand on the shoulders of others, with those that have come before us. In my life, words told to me, and writings that others have shared with me have mattered, and have impacted my life. In fact they have saved my sobriety and led me to a successful life.

It started really with my Parents. My father, as I've written before, was what the Irish playwright Sean O'Casey said of the Irish, "Those Beautiful, Brilliant fools" He was all of that, but his strong social conscience gave him also a love of poetry and philosophy. He was to make sure his children would too have a deep appreciation for the written word. Now his method of doing that could be debatable with my siblings, but with me it worked. My Mother, much more civil than my Father, was a deep believer in the gifts of Faith, Hope and Charity, believed in communication. Her belief was simple, we as individuals should always find the best way to communicate and understand people. It was like something we owed to society to make it better. So Prose and Poetry became stalwarts of my family's learning, and definitely something that I depended on to climb the career ladder, and most importantly stay sober.

Their writings inspired me. Whether it was the Greek philosophers: Socrates, Plato, or Aristotle, or the three great American Thinkers of Paine, Emerson, and King, or our Saints like Augustine, Francis, Thomas Aquinas, or Mother Theresa, their writings and sayings all had meaning, and gave a recovering alcoholic hope and stability. Then add some of our greatest poets like Shakespeare, Whitman, Frost, Sandburg, Dickinson, Angelou, Yeats, Joyce, Service, Thomas and Heaney and a whole new world of life's direction comes into focus. I learned to use their writings and their verse, as advice on how I should live, take risks, and as a result they replaced for me my AA 12 step program, and became my new 12 step livelihood. Or as Emerson said, "If our purpose in life is to sail to the Port of Heaven, then we must set our sails, Sometimes with the wind and sometimes against. But Not lay at bay at anchor" Do you remember the old saying, "To thine own self be true." Whether it came directly from the Bible as many scholars would argue, or right out of Shakespeare's play called Hamlet, it had great meaning In my life. I tried to follow that statement religiously. I attended over 300 AA meetings but left the group after 3-4 years, as I no longer felt I fit in, at least so I thought. But, I kept my anonymity and kept chatting with my sponsor. My sobriety brother and dear sponsor Jim, saw how I was struggling and he told me a story that I have never forgotten. He said, "You have to remember, we have two kinds of recovered alcoholics, Mike. The first group needs God's daily presence and forgiveness as they are afraid of going to hell, and we pray they find it. The second, doesn't need that, but are spiritually recovering alcoholics and not fearful of hell, as they have already been there and came through it." And that was me, and Jim knew it. He then told the story of the three great philosophers that have impacted his life, and helped keep him sober for Seven years back then. First, was Socrates, who taught us to Know thyself, second was Aristotle, who taught us to Understand thyself, and the third, and the greatest philosopher of them all was Christ, and he taught us to Give of thyself." How I loved that man, as he and what he said, had a great meaning in my life. He had a tremendous impact on me. And so I began to put my youths' learned experiences from my parents, and tied itself to my latest truth in philosophy from my sponsor Jim. I started reading and never stopped. I memorized songs and poems, read the greatest speeches ever given, and learned sayings of our own greatest philosophers. I even read the entire Bible, both new and old testaments, and most of Shakespeare's plays. The AA foundation of a 'higher power' acceptance was critical to my sobriety. So, I wanted to learn more about Christ, Mohammed, Buddha, and the Gitche Manitou. I applied everything told to me and everything I studied and read and memorized into my professional career in economic development as well as my fundraising career. One of the greatest quotes I read back in my early sobriety and career years was, "if you can dream it, you can achieve it". And I lived it. And so, as I started my business career, I worked to rebuild a life near ruin. It was when we all celebrated my first year sobriety, my life found itself secure in who I was, and what I was becoming. My Mother gave me another poem, and it meant the world to me, coming from her. Sober, at that celebration now for a year, I enjoyed her giving me, 'The Birth of an Irishman.' What a gift. I loved it. It said so much to me. My Mother finally accepted, respected and acknowledged her second son I felt. It always was her way but I foolishly never understood it. I thank God for her.

The Birth of an Irishman

Once there was a man,

Who pondered what to be.

He loved his piece of land,

And loved his bit of sea.

He could work like big men do,

Or frolick like a boy.

His eyes could flood with heartbreak,

His feet could dance with joy.

He could curse with the drunken men,

Or Warble with the lark.

Loving made him whisper,

And hating made him bark.

Part of him, was Angel,

And part the Devil's own,

At times, he walked with no one,

But he never walked alone.

And what did he become?

A Poet, a Pauper, a Prince?

He said No, I'll be an Irishman,

And he's charmed us ever since.

And as George Bernard Shaw once said, a life spent making mistakes is not only more honorable, but more useful than a life spent doing nothing. Let me share some of that life with you, my 50 year work career journey, and my 51 years of my sobriety. My Road to Sobriety has not ended, I'm still on that sober highway, and I have learned that gratitude is the healthiest of all human emotions. I am so grateful. Now how about you?

ENCLOSURES

THE TWELVE STEPS OF ALCOHOLICS ANONYMOUS

1. We admitted we were powerless over alcohol—that our lives had become unmanageable.

2. Came to believe that a Power greater than ourselves could restore us to sanity.

3. Made a decision to turn our will and our lives over to the care of God as we understood Him.

4. Made a searching and fearless moral inventory of ourselves.

5. Admitted to God, to ourselves, and to another human being the exact nature of our wrongs.

6. We're entirely ready to have God remove all these defects of character.

7. Humbly asked Him to remove our shortcomings.

8. Made a list of all persons we had harmed, and became willing to make amends to them all.

9. Made direct amends to such people wherever possible, except when to do so would injure them or others.

10. Continued to take personal inventory and when we were wrong promptly admitted it.

11. Sought through prayer and meditation to improve our conscious contact with God as we understood Him, praying only for knowledge of His will for us and the power to carry that out.

12. Having had a spiritual awakening as the result of these steps, we tried to carry this message to alcoholics, and to practice these principles in all our affairs.

FAQ - Most Frequently Asked Questions

- **What is the AA statement of anonymity?**

The name Alcoholics Anonymous assures you that your anonymity will be respected. In return, we ask that any names, or stories, that you hear here today be kept in confidence when you leave the premises. What you hear here, Whom you see here, Let it remain here, When you leave here!

- **How important is anonymity in AA?**

The purpose of anonymity is to protect members' identities so they can feel safe sharing their stories and experiences without fear of judgment or retaliation. It also helps to create a sense of equality among members, as everyone is on the same level regardless of their profession, social status, or other factors.

- **What is the difference between an open meeting and a closed meeting?**

Open meetings are available to anyone interested in Alcoholics Anonymous's program of recovery from alcoholism. Nonalcoholics may attend open meetings as observers. Closed meetings are for A.A. members only or for those who have a drinking problem and "have a desire to stop drinking."

- **What is the key to a good meeting?**

Plan and structure meetings.

All meetings need some structure, so publish the objective and an agenda up front even if it's just a few key bullet points (with guideline time slots, ideally). Pick a sensible timeframe but err on the short side; typically, meetings will fill the time allocated.

- **Will I be able to participate in the meeting?**

There are many opportunities to participate in various parts of an A.A. meeting. Each is a way to begin to connect with others and the group.

Many meetings will take a moment to allow visitors or newcomers to introduce themselves. This is not to embarrass or call anyone out; it is simply an opportunity for others in the meeting to get to know you. Remember, everyone was new once.

- **What is the difference between AA and AL-ANON**

AA, or Alcoholics Anonymous, is an international support group for individuals with a drinking problem. This non-professional, self-supporting organization has no age or education requirements. Meetings, with the exception of private meetings for those with alcoholism alone, are open to anyone who wishes to join. There are open and closed versions of meetings; while anyone can attend open gatherings, the closed meetings are reserved for members. The only qualification to be a member of AA is to have a drinking problem and the desire to stop drinking permanently.

Al-Anon, contrastingly, is designed for family members of individuals with alcohol problems. The name comes from the first syllables of Alcoholics Anonymous, 'al' and 'anon.' This type of meeting helps spouses, parents, siblings, and other family members of people who have an alcohol dependence. The only requirement to attend these meetings is to have someone close in your life who is an alcoholic.

While Al-Anon meetings may be spiritual, they are not rooted in any religion. Meetings will usually involve discussion of a certain topic related to having a loved one with an addiction. Topics of Al-Anon meetings may include:

- Acceptance

- Alcohol as a disease

- Making choices

- Changing attitudes

- Dealing with change

- Coping with anger

- Gaining courage

- Dealing with crises

- Denial issues

- Detachment

- Enabling

- Feelings of emptiness

- Importance of forgiveness

- Focusing one oneself

- Honesty

- Self esteem

Both AA and Al-Anon are support groups. However, AA is for people struggling with or recovering from alcohol use disorder, while Al-Anon is for people whose family members have histories of alcohol use disorder. Although addiction affects each group differently, there are some similarities, such as:

- Both groups provide support for those experiencing issues with alcohol abuse, whether their own or that of a loved one.

- Both groups nod to anonymity in their titles because the information shared in the rooms is not divulged to the general public.

- Both groups are free and open to the public.

- Both groups are meant to allow people to come to terms with the effects of addiction and talk with people who can relate.

Therefore, the main distinct difference between AA and Al-Anon is the audience that they serve.

- **How does Al-Anon and Alateen work?**

The Al-Anon and Alateen Twelve Steps are closely aligned to those of AA. The basic principle of the model is that people can help heal each other—but only if they surrender to a higher power.

It is important to remember that Al-Anon and Alateen are not treatment programs. Instead, they are about sharing personal experiences so that other members can find strength and consider how they might apply those lessons to their own lives. Alateen focuses on ages 12-19.

As with Alcoholics Anonymous (AA), Al-Anon and
Alateen are closely based on a 12-step model (known,
aptly, as the Twelve Steps), which is designed as a "tool for
spiritual growth."

- **What does an AA sponsor do?**

A sponsor is a senior member of AA who has been in recovery
for usually at least a year. Sponsors help you navigate
membership, answer questions, work on the 12-steps, and
offer accountability. A sponsor is also a confidant who understand where you have been.

Unlike a counselor, sponsors do not offer any formal therapy.
Their job is to be a supportive friend, someone you can
confide in and discuss feelings and thoughts you may not
always feel comfortable revealing in group therapy or at a
meeting. There are no requirements to be a sponsor.

The beauty of sponsorship is that it unites people from every
walk of life who have struggled with addiction. They have
stood in the shoes of the person they're sponsoring. Being a
sponsor is a volunteer role, but it consumes as much time and
energy as a full-time job.

Benefits of a 30-Day Addiction Treatment Program

There are many reasons to consider a 30-day alcohol and drug rehab treatment program. People who are struggling with a substance use disorder will greatly benefit from month-long treatment programs. Finding a rehab facility that caters to each patient's needs will provide the most benefit to individuals.

Benefits include:

- Opportunities to address and overcome any uncertainty related to treatment

- The opportunity to fully detox from drugs or alcohol

- Various therapies and counseling help individuals develop coping skills for dealing with cravings and triggers

- The chance to form lasting relationships with others in recovery from addiction

- Education on drug and alcohol addiction and how it affects a person's life and health

- A place to focus solely on recovery without distractions or temptations.

- While 30-day treatment programs certainly offer many benefits, this type of treatment is not for everyone. Individuals with more severe substance use disorders will likely need to attend a longer rehab program. Additionally, people suffering from health conditions as a result of drug or alcohol use may need more advanced care.

ACKNOWLEDGMENT

Thank you to everyone who have asked me to write a book of my Sobriety Journey. I hope it can reach out and hopefully touch a family, or touch an individual suffering from addiction. Be they old or young, or to a group that have been struck down with addiction to alcohol, I hope this book brings you hope, and lights a fire within your soul. I've mentioned several times in the book, my sponsor, my friends, my colleagues at work, and my boss, all those who were directly involved in keeping me on the sober highway. The beauty of it is there were several people who believed enough in me to hang tough when things were extremely hard for them as well. I was lucky, and as my Dad used to say, "You have to be good to be lucky." The other old saying was, "there's nothing worse than a dried up drunk", I'm sure it was very true with me, especially that first and second year of my sobriety. I experienced personality changes, dry drunks, several horrible nightmares, and several days of just being high with life. All of this with no meds, as my ulcers were healing finally. But, I did make a few mistakes those first few years, I was married to a lovely girl, but it happened right after I quit drinking. Professionals told both of us to take our time, enjoy what was happening, but, just wait and see how things go. The point being was, I was new to sobriety. She had no idea who she really was marrying. The facts are still facts, I never would have made it through without her, and although our marriage didn't work, I will always highly regard her and thank her for my three children and getting me and keeping me on my road to sobriety. If one thought alcoholism is tough to overcome, well so too is a divorce, especially on children. It was always my goal when I sobered up that not one of my children would ever see their father drunk. They didn't. And there never was a 3 am wake up call in their youth. I kept that promise but I still had the characteristics of an alcoholic, regardless of me being sober or not. I failed as a husband, but I remain committed to being a loving and caring father, and now my adult children have their own challenges. The answer isn't a simple one, but yes, they too have come from a dysfunctional family, but on the day they were born and I was there, they were born into love. Never to be forgotten were my Mothers prayers. I have used this recommendation so often in my 12 step work, that there is nothing more powerful than a Mother's prayers. And they work.

Of course my family were very supportive, and helpful. But the inside struggle of an alcoholic family still existed. At that time the night terrors existed now for my younger brother Tim, and he was by himself with Mom. He was a tough little guy, and grew up to be a wonderful man. I've asked him on several occasions, were there any scars left with him growing up in this madness. He was cut right down the middle between John and Kathy on one side, who were similar in many ways and the other side was with Mary and Myself, as we were a lot alike. So he was able to manage his life better than his older siblings. However, I always wished I would have been there for him. I was proud of the fact though that My Road to Sobriety had its impact on the family, but it moved very slowly.

It was during the early years of being sober, I met once again my Jesuit priest friend, Fr. B, a lovely man with a great sense of humor, and a recovered alcoholic himself, and a lovely older American Indian woman named Verna. Years after we met, she ran for US Congress and became the first woman to be elected Mayor of the Soo, that was quite an honor. She was unique. Anyway, I coached her son in football when he was in high school, but how we first met is worth telling. Her husband, was a kind and gentle man, a friendly mailman, but after work he loved his drink at Hallesy's Bar. As you know now, that was my home away from home. Well we had a few drinks together with friendly chat, and that led to a few more drinks, and still a few more. Now I had a special knack for getting people very angry at me after I had to much to drink, and was told by several of my friends that I could even make Christ swear at me. I truly don't recall what I said to him, but he followed me into the bathroom and we got in a scuffle in the men's facility. All I remember is being hit, and then I grabbed him and dunked his head into the toilet bowl filled with everything imaginable, and flushed it while I held him down. Then I walked out and left him there. The next day at work I was sitting at my desk, of course hungover, when the Mrs. came yelling into our offices asking, "where the hell is Mike McCarthy"? The secretary brought her down to my office and I had my hands holding my head up over the desk, and I met her for the first time. She yelled, she screamed really at me and asked if I was the SOB that beat up her husband? I raised my head and took my hands off over my eyes and she said, "OMG what happened to you." All I needed to show her was my face, as I had two black-eyes where her husband hit me and broke my glasses. She couldn't believe it was her husband, but I assured her it was and I told her what I did, and I said I hope he's ok. She went on for the next half hour that we chatted, and said she had been cleaning up her husband for hours, taking cigarettes and toilet paper out of his hair, his nose, his ears and how he smelled of urine. That's how we met and later on in my sobriety she called me and asked if I would do some 12 step work with him and I did. He and I became good friends, and a few years later he did find his own sobriety. But anyway, Fr. B and Verna, took me under their wing and coached me, encouraged me and became a major part of my life. As I think of them today, and I think of them often, I thank them and love them so much still.

And finally, thanks to the hundreds and hundreds of recovering alcoholics I met in AA and in my professional life. Their anonymity will always be protected. I want to thank them for allowing a moment or two in their life, to speak up at meetings. Being vulnerable and trusting the process can be difficult, but they did it. You gave me hope and lit a fire within me to stay on My Road to Sobriety. I know now after 51 years, if you're reading this and suffering, wondering, denying, or seeking help, you can achieve a sober life. It won't come easy, but take one day at a time, and before you know it, you too will celebrate your first month being sober. Then six months, then a year. I know you can do it. It all begins with this - Admitting you are powerless over alcohol—that your life has become unmanageable. And as my Father said to me a thousand times, "there can be no happiness in life, if what we believe in, is different than what we do". I believe you can find your sobriety, now it's up to you. Good luck!

Two months before my Mother died she sent me one last poem, and I share it with you, because it also was meant for you reading this book. It's called, 'Go Climb that Mountain'.

Go Climb That Mountain

(Jenny Phillips/Tyler Castleton)

Go climb that mountain, go climb that mountain

If you start with willing feet you can conquer anything

Set your feet on that road and go

Every time you cast your eyes on that mountain

It seems the peaks reach further than the skies

But that mountain was made for your feet

And there's one that has always believed in your journey

Trust that God has sent you here with the power

To conquer things that seem beyond your reach

It's not going to move on its own, but you don't have to do it alone

He is with you

Go climb that mountain, go climb that mountain

If you start with willing feet you can conquer anything

Set your feet on that road and go, go climb that mountain

McCARTHY FAMILY PICTURES

Friends for life, my sister Mary and Barbara Hallesy.

Reverend Peter G Campbell, and wife Julie. Great friends, authored the Books Foreword. Outstanding hockey player in his time.

My Sisters. Kathy and Mary

My Father walking Kathy down the aisle, 1971.

To his memory, John T McCarthy, Son, Brother, Father, Husband. May 23, 1945 - October 7, 2016, RIP.

1910 the McCarthy Mill

Our Family, Myself, Judy and our little golden doodle Gracie.

My wife Judy and myself

My brother Tim

My sister Mary's painting of our Grama Trempe.

My Grandfather Pop, as a young man, married August 1, 1915.

My dearest friend in life, Marie O'Connor and Mike.

My dear friend Verna Lawrence

Celebrating John's 70th birthday. Left to Right, Mary, Mike, Tim, Kathy, Jean, and John.

**Six months before her marriage to my Father. -
Frances at work at Ma Bell, 1943.**

**My Father, John T. McCarthy. June 1939
Graduation from Hugh School.**

The O'Connor Family, Tipperary, Ireland. Front Row, Seamus, Mrs. O'Connor, Val, Back row, Geraldine, Marie, Caitriona.

The McCarthy's, L to R, Mike, Mary, Tim, Kathy and John

My Mother - Frances Martha McCarthy

Mom At her 75th Birthday

1962 John's Graduation - Dad and John

My Sponsor Jim Fenlon

TESTIMONIALS

Well… here we go… it's sounds like a Confessional. The story is finally told for many of us, and this is how we lived, and survived. Our die was cast, from jr high onward. You and Pete make me very proud of both of you.

- Tim Kinney

"As one who comes from a long line of saloon keepers and alcoholics, I endorse this recovery story. It reaches the hard working drinkers who struggle with addiction. Inspiration saves lives.
It's never too early or too late."

- Barb Hallesy Wirt

"As I look back on our lives together, the disease of alcoholism was part of our lives, but with the help and support of my husband's life long friend Mike, our family was able to flourish. Mike was there to support Tim when he was at his lowest point. Our family was able to live a very healthy and happy life together.

- Patty Madigan McCasey

I never knew you were that close to death, Mike. What a story and what a book, Congratulations. I couldn't put the book down, once I started reading it. Thank you for choosing to live, and thank you for helping, me and my family.

- David Rieger

"Quite a trip through our crazy times Mac. Congratulations to both you and Pete for your strength and endurance. I, as well, am proud we are all friends to the end."

- Fred Benoit

"I have known and worked with Michael for 20 years, I can attest to his storytelling prowess and his practice of helping others. This book is a remarkably frank and engaging, and it will inspire everyone who reads it."

- Susan Blansett

"I'm sure many people across the country will be able to identify with your struggles. A brave story has been told!"

- Connie Jaros Drake

"This naive Italian-American Catholic classmate of Mike's, who was never touched by alcoholism in my own family, was brought to tears reading this book. How could my naivete have blinded me to what my friends were living through? My prayer is that each person reads slowly and carefully with an open heart this book."

- Angie Bonacci Morehouse